全国高职高专专业英语规划教材

营销英语

（第2版）

李冬梅 主　编
谭英　蒋霞　韦爱云　副主编
[新西兰] John Nelson 审　阅

清华大学出版社
北　京

内容简介

本书选取了营销的 16 个核心概念，内容涉及营销管理理念、战略计划、营销环境、消费者市场与消费者购买行为，组织市场与组织购买行为、市场细分、选择目标市场和市场定位、产品和服务战略、产品定价方法、定价策略、分销渠道等各个方面。

本书共设 16 个单元，每单元围绕一个核心概念展开 4~5 个问题，每部分围绕一个特定的问题进行阐述或引导学生讨论运用。

本书可作为高等院校市场营销及相关专业的英语教材或双语教材，也可作为相关人员的培训或阅读材料。

本书封面贴有清华大学出版社防伪标签，无标签者不得销售。
版权所有，侵权必究。举报：010-62782989，beiqinquan@tup.tsinghua.edu.cn。

图书在版编目 (CIP) 数据

营销英语 / 李冬梅主编. —2 版. —北京：清华大学出版社，2018（2022.8重印）
（全国高职高专专业英语规划教材）
ISBN 978-7-302-45418-2

Ⅰ. ①营… Ⅱ. ①李… Ⅲ. ①市场营销学—英语—高等职业教育—教材 Ⅳ. ① H31

中国版本图书馆 CIP 数据核字 (2016) 第 260147 号

责任编辑：陈立静
装帧设计：杨玉兰
责任校对：张文青
责任印制：刘海龙

出版发行：清华大学出版社
网　　址：http://www.tup.com.cn, http://www.wqbook.com
地　　址：北京清华大学学研大厦 A 座　　邮　编：100084
社 总 机：010-83470000　　邮　购：010-62786544
投稿与读者服务：010-62776969, c-service@tup.tsinghua.edu.cn
质量反馈：010-62772015, zhiliang@tup.tsinghua.edu.cn
课件下载：http://www.tup.com.cn, 010-62791865

印 装 者：天津鑫丰华印务有限公司
经　　销：全国新华书店
开　　本：185mm×260mm　　印　张：11.75　　字　数：200 千字
版　　次：2010 年 4 月第 1 版　2018 年 6 月第 2 版　印　次：2022 年 8 月第 5 次印刷
定　　价：46.00 元

产品编号：072448-01

　　随着经济全球化进程的加快及市场竞争的加剧，中国对既掌握营销的理念与知识、又能熟练运用英语进行交流的人才的需求不断上升。高职高专的教育更应面向市场，强调知识的应用性及可操作性。因此，本教材将营销的理念与策略融入英语学习中，强调营销理论的实践性及英语的应用性，引导学生在用中学、在学中用，集知识性、体验性和应用性为一体。

　　在内容的编排上，本书选取了营销的16个核心概念，每个单元围绕一个核心概念展开4～5个问题，每部分围绕一个特定的问题阐述或引导学生讨论运用。通过对这16个核心概念的学习，学生能够对"营销是什么，为什么营销，营销有什么用"基本了然于胸。

　　本书以"基于内容的语言学习法"(content-based language learning) 为指导方针。在语言输入上充分考虑到高职高专学生的普遍水平，强调"可理解性输入"，尽量选取表达简洁清晰、适合专科学生阅读的文章。每单元设计的活动，基本都要求学生课外动手查找资料，这样既有利于知识的拓展，又可提高学生的参与性。每一章设计的案例翻译题，要求学生首先将中文翻译成英文，然后结合该章学习的内容，用英文讨论案例的思考题。本书提供的16个案例是以几个年轻人创业为主线串联而成的一个完整故事，配合每章学习的内容撰写。通过对案例的翻译和讨论，培养学生用英文表达自己思想的能力，提高学生用学过的理论解决实际问题的能力，同时激发他们积极思考的学习热情。

　　在量的设计上，本书适用于一个学期、每周2～3个学时的课程安排。在理想情况下，以每学期18周计算，大约每周可完成一个单元的教学。考虑到国家节假日对

课时可能的冲减以及各个学校生源的不同情况，本书各章特别设计了补充材料，教师可根据实际情况选用，适当调整教学进度。

  与一般的语言类教材不同的是，本书没有提供生词表，只是对某些需要背景知识才能理解的词汇进行了相应的注释。这样设置有如下两个原因：其一，现在的字典无论是从种类还是功能上都比以前更为丰富全面，尤其是网络字典，更是方便快捷，学生完全可以自己查字典。一个单词可能有很多种意思，学生真正需要思考的是某个单词在具体语境下是什么意思。只有通过自己动手查阅并加以思考，对一个单词的记忆才会深刻。其二，本书没有在每一篇阅读材料后提供阅读理解问题，这样可以给教师留出一些发挥的空间。根据编者的教学体会，有些教材编得很全面，将问题都设计好了，教师完全按照编者的思路来执行（不是设计）教学活动，主观能动性未能得到发挥，学生也觉得老师照本宣科，没有新鲜感，使得教学效果不够理想。因此，本书设计的问题大多需要学生拓展课本知识（不仅仅是阅读理解），自己动手查找资料，将课内学习与课外动手相结合才能完成学习任务。问题大都没有标准答案，意在鼓励学生独立思考、勇于发表个人见解。

  本书在编写过程中参考了很多资料，在此要特别感谢本书参考资料的作者，他们的智慧加上编者作为一线教师的经验，才使本书得以面世。

编　者

Unit 1　The Marketing Concept ································ 1

Unit 2　The Marketing Environment ···························· 10

Unit 3　Marketing Research ····································· 24

Unit 4　Target Market ··· 37

Unit 5　New Product Development ······························ 45

Unit 6　Branding ·· 57

Unit 7　Packaging ··· 70

Unit 8　Pricing ·· 85

Unit 9　Distribution ··· 100

Unit 10　Advertising ·· 109

Unit 11　Sales Promotion ······································· 119

Unit 12　Public Relations ······································· 128

Unit 13　Personal Selling ······································· 137

Unit 14　On-line Marketing ····································· 147

Unit 15　International Marketing ································ 156

Unit 16　Green Marketing ······································ 169

Unit 1

The Marketing Concept

After learning this unit, you will be able to answer the following questions.

- How can we make customers satisfied?
- What is marketing?
- Shall we satisfy any needs of customers?
- What is the role of marketing and what do marketers do?

Marketing

Warm-up Activities

Top producers today realize they can no longer get by on product expertise alone. They know the real expert is the customer.

——*Linda Richardson*

What's your understanding of the above saying? How important do you think customers are to a business?

 Reading 1

What Is Marketing?

What does the term "marketing" mean? Most people think of marketing only as selling and advertising. And no wonder everyday we are surrounded with television commercials, newspaper ads and billboard slogans. However, selling and advertising are only the tip of the marketing iceberg.

Marketing is a process of finding out the needs and wants of the market then designing products or services to satisfy these needs and wants in order to achieve organizational objectives. To make it simple, marketing is getting the right goods and services to the right people at the right time, at the right place, at the right price, with the right communication.

Normally we think a market is a place where buyers and sellers gather to exchange their goods and services. More importantly, a market is the set of actual and potential buyers (customers) of a product or service. These buyers (customers) share a particular need or want that can be satisfied through exchanges and relationships.

A market is made up of people with both the desire and the ability to buy a specific product. All markets ultimately are people. Even when we say a firm bought a Xerox copier, we mean one or several people in the firm decided to buy it. People who are aware of their unmet needs may have the desire to buy the product, but that isn't sufficient. People must also have the ability to buy, such as the authority, time and money.

Essentially, marketing is the process of creating or directing an organization to be successful in selling a product or service that people not only desire, but are willing to buy.

Therefore good marketing must be able to create a set of benefits for customers by delivering value through products or services.

(Adapted from Philip Kotler, et al. *Principles of Marketing*, Pearson Education Australia, 2006, Chapter 1.)

Concept Check

1. Marketing is a process which starts from _____ and ends with _____.

2. A market is formed by a group of people who have both the _____ and _____ to buy a product or _____.

 Reading 2

The Role of Marketing

As we've seen, the key objective of an organization's marketing efforts is to develop satisfying relationships with customers that benefit both the customers and the organization. These efforts lead marketing to serve as an important role within most organizations and within a society.

At the organizational level, marketing is a vital business function that is necessary in nearly all industries whether the organization operates as a for-profit or as a not-for-profit unit. For the for-profit organization, marketing is responsible for most tasks that bring revenue and, hopefully, profits to an organization. For the not-for-profit organization, marketing is responsible for attracting customers needed to support the not-for-profit mission, such as raising donations or supporting a cause. For both types of organizations, it is unlikely they can survive without a strong marketing effort.

Marketing is also the organizational business area that interacts most frequently with the public and, consequently, what the public knows about an organization is determined by their interactions with marketers. For example, customers may believe a company is dynamic and creative based on its advertising message.

At a broader level marketing offers significant benefits to society. These benefits include the following.

● Developing products that satisfy needs, including products that enhance society's quality of life.

● Creating a competitive environment that helps lower product prices.

● Developing product distribution systems that offer access to products to a large number of customers and many geographic regions.

● Building demand for products that require organizations to expand their labor force.

● Offering techniques that have the ability to convey messages that change societal behavior in a positive way (e.g. anti-smoking advertising).

(From http://www.projectsandmarketing.com/Rol.html)

Application

1. Describe how the following products improve the quality of your life.

Product	How they improve the quality of my life
Mobile phone	It helps me…
Computer	
Camera	
Washing machine	

2. China Mobile and China Unicom are two giants in the Chinese telecommunication market. As a mobile phone user, how can you benefit from the competition of these two companies?

3. You go into a supermarket in your city and you can find products coming from different parts of China, even different parts of the world. The kinds of organization listed below help the product reach your hands. Please translate the terms into English, and find an example of each kind from real life.

Chinese	English	Example
批发商		
零售商		Wal-Mart
进口商		
出口商		
代理商		
货运公司		
保险公司		
海关		

4. Besides the anti-smoking advertising, do you know of any advertisement that does not sell a product but educates people? Share one with your classmates.

Activity 1

How Can We Make Customers Satisfied?

1. You have bought a computer from a local shop and you are very satisfied with the computer. List the reasons below to tell why you are satisfied.

_____

_____

_____

_____

2. Marketing is a process of making customers satisfied. But how do you make customers satisfied? Let's have a look at how Lands' End does its business.

Lands' End is a direct merchant of traditionally styled clothing for the family, soft luggage, and products for the home. (For detailed information, please visit www.landsend.com.)

The Lands' End Principles of Doing Business (excerpted)

Principle 1

We do everything we can to make our products better. We improve material, and add back features and construction details that others have taken out over the years. We never reduce the quality of a product to make it cheaper.

Principle 2

We price our products fairly and honestly.

Principle 3

We accept any return for any reason, at any time.

Principle 4

We ship faster than anyone we know of. We ship items in stock the day after we receive the order.

Principle 5

We believe that what is best for our customer is best for all of us. Everyone here understands that concept. Our sales and service people are trained to know our products, and to be friendly and helpful. They are urged to take all the time necessary to take care of you. We even pay for your call, for whatever reason you call.

Now work in groups and discuss the ways of satisfying customers by completing the following table.

To satisfy customers, your **product** must be	
To satisfy customers, your **price** must be	
To satisfy customers, your **delivery** must be	
To satisfy customers, your **service** must be	

 **Activity 2**

Should We Satisfy Any Needs of our Customers?

News Report

From June 1, 2008, all Chinese retailers, including supermarkets, department stores and grocery stores, no longer provide free plastic shopping bags. China will try to reduce the use of plastic bags in a bid to reduce energy consumption and polluting emissions.

Think it Over

People need	Reasons for not satisfying this need
Plastic bags	
Cigarettes	
Disposable chopsticks	
Luxurious packaging for moon-cakes	

In an age of environmental problems, resource shortages, and rapid population growth, there is a strong call for an organization to be socially responsible.

One such company is Nokia. Nokia's environmental work is based on life cycle thinking. It does everything to minimize the environmental impact of its products throughout operations, beginning with the extraction of raw materials and ending with recycling, treatment of waste, and recovery of used materials. It achieves this by better product design, close control of the production processes, and greater material reuse and recycling.

Application

Visit the web pages of the following companies and find out the socially responsible activities they have implemented.

Company Name	Socially Responsible Activities
STARBUCKS COFFEE http://www.starbucks.com/responsibility	

 http://www.kfc.com/about/responsibility.asp	
 http://www.microsoft.com/environment/	
 http://www.samsung.com/cn/aboutsamsung/ citizenship/usactivities.html	

Activity 3

Translation and Discussion (1)

Translate the following story and the questions into English, and then discuss the questions in English.

韩柳、开朗和志成是高中同学。高中毕业后，韩柳考上了一所重点大学学习市场营销，现在东莞的一家制鞋公司做销售员。开朗学的是服装设计，毕业后没有找固定的工作，而是花了不少时间到处旅游。按她的话说是要去寻找生活中的服装元素。志成没有考上大学，在本地的一家百货公司做售货员。

受金融危机的影响，韩柳所在的公司倒闭了，她只好回到了自己的家乡。一天，三个好朋友相聚，韩柳突然萌生了三个人一同创业的想法。

问题
1. 如果他们三个真要自主创业，你认为他们做什么比较合适呢？
2. 如果他们决定自主创业，首先要考虑的是什么？

Importance of Marketing

—Scott F. Geld

Marketing is a broad topic that covers a range of aspects, including advertising, public relations, sales, and promotions. People often confuse sales with marketing, when in fact the two are very different. The former involves getting a product or service into the market, promoting it, influencing behavior, and encouraging sales. Sales are the actual transaction of getting a product or service into the hands of your customers.

Strategies in marketing have changed enormously since Jay Conrad Levinson introduced the guerrilla concept over 20 years ago. Tactics that were considered radical then are almost main stream now. With so many messages bombarding the consumer in the marketplace today, it is now more difficult than ever to get your product noticed, so marketers have learned to be creative.

Companies without a marketing mindset are at a disadvantage in today's business world. Those who are still centered around their products, rather than their customers, are doomed to fail.

Knowing what your clients' expectations are, exceeding them, and building a reputation based on that is the key to success. Pay attention to your customers, and they will come back time and time again. Ignore them, and they will disappear faster than you can spend your marketing budget to try to bring them back.

Many people do not know much about marketing and they always feel that the marketing staff in the company is a burden on the company and they do not justify the dollars spent on them. But the fact is that sincere marketing efforts never go to waste. When you invest in marketing related activities, you are sure to reap benefits. Well run marketing campaigns can help you earn good profits.

Some people have a misconception about the term marketing, they feel that it is an easy task and anyone can do it. But as a business person you have to get rid of this view point and employ a professional marketing agency that will devise your marketing strategy and help you execute it as well. Or you can also have the assistance of an independent marketing consultant who can oversee the marketing efforts that are being put in by the marketing department.

The outside marketing agency or the professional marketing consultant will be able to focus on all the company's marketing requirements without being bothered by aspects like internal company politics or employee relationships, etc.

These professionals are very aware of the strategies that work for various products and the strategies that will not work. For devising your marketing strategies you definitely should take assistance from these marketing professionals.

About The Author

Scott F. Geld is the Executor of Marketing Blaster, a pay-per-click traffic source that continually beats the other major search engines in conversion ratio and ROI. See for yourself at *http://www.marketingblaster.com*.

Questions

1. Is marketing becoming more and more popular in China? What marketing activities have you seen in daily life?

2. Can you list the reasons for learning marketing in modern society, especially in the fast developing China?

Unit 2

The Marketing Environment

After learning this unit, you will be able to answer the following questions.

- How can a company react to the marketing environment?
- What is marketing environment?
- What elements are involved in a macroenvironment?
- What are the characteristics of the marketing environment?
- What elements are involved in a microenvironment?
- How can the marketing environment be categorized?

Marketing Environment

Warm-up Activities

In what way do you think the following pictures may affect our life or business? Suppose you want to set up your own business, which of them may affect your decision? Why?

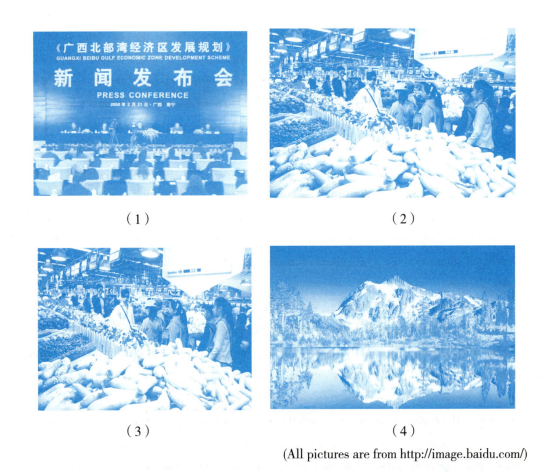

(1)   (2)

(3)   (4)

(All pictures are from http://image.baidu.com/)

 Reading 1

The Marketing Environment (I)—Microenvironment

Definition

Everything happens or operates in a certain environment. As an environment generally refers to the external situations and conditions of a matter, the **marketing environment** refers to all outside factors and conditions related to the marketing activities of an organization. These factors and conditions are constituted by the forces outside a company and they affect the company's ability to maintain successful relationships with its target customers, thus they affect its global and domestic marketing efforts. While making use of the material and information resources from the environment around, a company also influences the outside world by putting out products, labor and information, and the marketing activities can facilitate the interactions of the company's internal and external resources.

Nature of the Marketing Environment

We will first look into the distinctive features of the marketing environment.

First, the marketing environment is **objective**. Objectivity is the most outstanding feature of marketing environment. The existence and function of an environment is objective so that any organization should direct its marketing strategies according to the objective trend of the environment, otherwise its blind plan or decision will lead to inconceivable failures in the future.

Second, it is **dynamic**. Like any other type of environment, marketing environment is not a static one. Any marketing environment will change with the change of any factor involved, such as the consuming need and purchasing power of customers, the change of population or even any variation in the political policy in a place.

Third, it is **uncontrollable**. Elements of the marketing environment are largely uncontrollable, although marketers can influence marketing activities. For example, the condition of suppliers, the social culture or the legal and political situation is not controllable to an organization.

Classification of the Marketing Environment

According to the way and the degree of its influence on an organization, marketing environment falls into two major categories: the microenvironment (also known as direct environment) and the macroenvironment (also known as indirect environment). The microenvironment consists of the forces close to the company that affect its ability to serve its customers—the company, suppliers, marketing channel firms, competitors, and publics. The macroenvironment consists of the larger societal forces that affect the microenvironment—demographic, economic, natural, technological, political, and cultural forces. The relationship of macroenviroment, microenvironment and the companys' marketing activities can be shown in Exhibit2.1.

Exhibit 2.1

As both types of environment are vital to an organization, it is inadvisable for any company to ignore either of the two types. And in the following section, we will first focus on the discussion of microenvironment of an organization.

The Company's Microenvironment

The companys' microenvironment is directly connected with its economic benefits and directly influences the marketing services of the company. It consists of groups and organizations of the following six broad categories—the company itself, suppliers, marketing intermediaries, target customers, competitors and publics, which can be shown in Exhibit 2.2 as below.

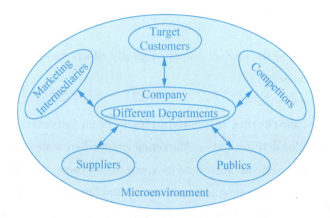

Exhibit 2.2

● The Company

To attract and build relationships with customers by creating customer value and satisfaction is the focus of marketers, but to realize this aim, marketers cannot depend on the marketing department alone. They must work together with different departments of the company.

While designing their marketing plans, marketers have to consider other departments such as the **top management**, finance, research and development (R&D), purchasing, manufacturing and accounting.

First of all, the top management sets the company's mission, the general aim, strategies and policies, and the **marketing department** will figure out specific marketing plans according to the general ones from the top. Then, the marketing department will depend on the mutual efforts of all other departments to realize their marketing aim. The **finance** is responsible for the funds needed during any project; the **R& D** should design and develop new products that are popular in the market; the **manufacturing** is focusing on the production of the products; and the **accounting** deals with the relation of cost and income so as to provide evidences for the top management to evaluate whether or not they have reached the objective set beforehand.

● Suppliers

Suppliers refer to those enterprises or individuals that supply goods or services they manufacture or handle to the company. The influence that suppliers bear on the company can be reflected in the following aspects.

To begin with, the reliability of resource supply, i.e., the assurance for the supply of resources directly influences the sales volumes and delivery time.

Furthermore, the prices and the trend of the fluctuation of the prices are closely related to the cost of the company.

Finally, the quality of the products supplied greatly affects the quality of the company's products sold to its customers.

- Marketing Intermediaries

Like suppliers, **marketing intermediaries** form an important component of the company's over-all value delivery system. Marketing intermediaries are organizations that help the company to promote, sell, and distribute its goods to end users. They include middlemen, physical distribution firms, marketing service agencies, and financial intermediaries.

Middlemen such as wholesalers and /or retailers are those organizations or individuals that help the company to find final customers or directly deal with customers. Therefore, unless the company sets up its own marketing channels, the working efficiency and service quality will directly influence the selling conditions of the company's products.

Physical distribution firms are specialized organizations that help the company to stock and move goods from their original places to their destinations. They include warehouses and transportation firms, such as DHL, UPS, TNT, FEDEX, etc.

Marketing services agencies include marketing research firms, financing firms, advertising companies, various advertising media and marketing consultant firms, whose specialized services are indispensable to the company's marketing activities.

Financial intermediaries include banks, credit companies, insurance companies and other businesses that help finance transactions or insure against the risks associated with the buying and selling of goods. In the modern society, almost all companies are closely related to and deal with financing intermediaries. All the resources of loans, the fluctuation of the bank's interest for loans and the insurance rate of the insurance company affect the company's marketing activities.

- Target Customers

As objects of the company's services, **target customers** refer to the direct buyers and users of the company's products or services. The marketers' major aim is to effectively provide products and services to its target customers through their co-efforts with different forces in the marketing channels. The features and change of customers' needs are the focus of marketing activities. Thus, marketers need to study its customers closely.

● Competitors

No company can exist alone in a certain market, for total monopolization is seldom seen in the reality. Thus, the company's efforts in the market will encounter the influence of other similar firms who compete for the force of the same market. These firms form competitors of the company.

● Publics

Publics are any group that has an actual or potential interest in or influence on the company's ability to realize its marketing objectives. They include financing publics, media publics, government publics, community publics and internal publics. As these publics can both enhance or hinder the company's ability to achieve its marketing goals, and sometimes the attitudes of the publics will directly affect the marketing prospect of the company, thus, it is vital to appropriately deal with the publics. Nowadays, a lot of enterprises set up public departments whose function and influence will be discussed in details in Unit 12.

(Adapted from Gary Armstrong & Philip Kotler, *Marketing: An Introduction*, Prentice-Hall, Inc. 2000: 70.)

 Reading 2

The Marketing Environment (II)—Macroenvironment

Macroenvironment refers to the major social forces that operate through affecting the microenvironment of the company, including demographic environment, economic environment, natural environment, technological environment, sociocultural environment and political environment, as shown in Exhibit 2.3.

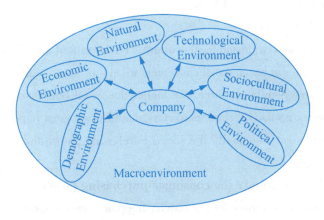

Exhibit 2.3

Through affecting different aspects of the microenvironment of the company, these social forces can both shape opportunities and pose threats to the company's marketing activities. The following parts of the unit will focus on effects of the company's marketing plans.

- Demographic Environment

The **demographic environment** is of major interest to marketers as it involves people, and it is people who make up markets. From a quantitative aspect, the number of people is an important symbol for the scale of a market. From the qualitative aspect, such as the analysis of the distribution, structure and changing trends of the population can reveal the features and developing tendency of the marketing needs. Then what are the features of demographic environment and how do they influence the company's marketing activities?

Firstly, the world population is growing rapidly. A growing population means growing human needs to satisfy. Depending on purchasing power, it may also mean growing market opportunities. China is considered to be "the most prosperous market of the 21st century", not only out of the rapid growth of its economy, but also due to the increasingly large population.

Secondly, the structure of the population also deserves attention. The structure of population that affects marketing plans can be analyzed from the natural structure (such as sex and age) and the social structure (such as living style, profession, nationality and family). When designing, packing and pushing the products into the market, marketers should take all these factors into consideration, so that the company can provide suitable products for different types of people. For example, exciting or adventurous activities should aim at youngsters, while medical care products should look for the old, and high-end cosmetic products should regard rich, elegant and well-educated ladies as target customers.

Lastly, the distribution of population is another aspect for attention. People in certain area may form different features of need and peculiar consuming habits, which can be proved by peculiar dishes in different areas of China.

- Economic Environment

International, national-wide and local **economic environment** are all critically significant to marketers, as people can become real consumers when they possess the necessary economic ability. With the same population force, the higher the social purchasing power, the larger the scale of marketing need. Therefore, marketers should place great importance on the trend of economic environment, especially the social purchasing power and the structure of the expenditure of the people.

First of all, they should take the **consumer purchasing power** into consideration. The income of consumers is the source for the purchasing power, including the consumers' salary, bonus, allowance, dividend, rent payment and all other styles of currency income. Usually, with the stability of commodity price, the higher income level tends to generate higher purchasing power and in turn more opportunities for the market.

In addition, marketers should look into the **consumer spending patterns** as well, i.e., the proportion of income used for food, housing, transportation, clothing, health care, entertainment, insurance and so on. Consumers at different income levels have different spending patterns, which were noted by Ernst Engel a century ago. Ernst Engel created the famous **Engel's laws** to indicate the proportion of food in a family's income. He pointed out that the bigger the coefficient, the poorer the economic state and vice versa.

Finally, marketers should pay attention to the global economic climate. In an age when faxes, phone lines and the Internet can instantaneously carry orders and information highway around the world to a waiting supplier or customer, every marketer is influenced by the global economic environment. The case that marketers have to adjust their marketing plans because of the financial crisis sweeping over the world since 2008 is well illustrative.

● Natural Environment

Natural environment is the fundamental activity space and material resources for human beings, and the change of natural environment is closely related to human activities. For marketers, the natural environment involves the natural resources available to or affected by the organization, such as air, water, minerals, plants, and animals. While a company uses some of these resources to produce its goods or provide its services, its activities also affect the natural surrounding environment. Therefore, marketers should be well aware of the current trends related to natural resources.

The first trend involves increasing shortage of raw materials. Even though there are infinite resources like air or water, the pollution of these resources poses great threats to many places in China and the world. Renewable resources such as forests and foodstuff should also be used with abstention, since the renewing cycle may take a considerable period of time. Nonrenewable resources like oil, coal and various minerals have caused serious problems. The shortage of natural resources has become a great obstacle or even counterforce to the economic development of various economies throughout the world.

The increasing pollution of the natural environment becomes the second trend. The development of industrialization and urbanization has caused increasing pollution of the natural environment such as the exhaustion of the natural resources, the pollution of the ocean, desertification of the soil, the harmful effects of green house and the crisis of biological environment. Nowadays, people's clear awareness of serious results brought by pollution constitutes great pressure for those enterprises that still pose great threats to the environment, while those industries that help control pollution by producing environmentally friendly products will be warmly welcome by the whole populace.

Marketers should also consider the government intervention in natural resources management. Any marketing activity running against the government policy will lead to failure.

Fortunately, people throughout the world have realized the importance of environmental protection, which brings about advanced marketing ideas such as "**sustainable development**" and "**green marketing**". These will be thoroughly discussed in Unit 16 of this book.

- Technological Environment

The **technological environment** includes factors and trends related to innovations that affect the development of new products or the marketing process. Rapid technological advances make it imperative that markets take a technological perspective. These new technological trends can provide opportunities for new-product development, affect how marketing activities are performed, or both.

Nowadays, people all over the world have clearly realized that science and technology is the first productivity and the 21st century is a new century for the further development of high technology. Therefore, marketers should seize the developing trends of technological revolution, attach great importance to the effects that the change of technological environment bears on marketing activities, and take appropriate measures accordingly.

Firstly, new technology creates new marketing opportunities and produces new industries. For example, with the development of technology in the computer science, the Internet and related industries grow quickly. Technological products can help marketers become more productive. Fax machines and mobile phones are good examples. On the other hand, new technology also poses threats to some industries. For example, laser discs have almost occupied the market of cassette tapes, and duplicating machines have taken that of carbon paper.

Secondly, enterprises benefit a lot in management with the use of new technology. New technology provides better sources and equipment and brings new ideas in the managing system of the company. Various types of devices designed for quality control are very illustrative.

Thirdly, the technological environment is characterized by rapid change. Most of today's common products that were not available 50 years ago, or even 20 years ago. For example, color TV sets just entered into Chinese households in the late 1980s, and the appearance of smart phones were in 2000.

Fourthly, the development of new technology influences the company's decisions in making marketing strategies. The new technology shortens the production period which causes the company to develop new products constantly. The advanced telecommunication technology and multi-media publicizing make the advertising industry more influential.

Finally, new technology has changed the structure of retailing and consumers' shopping habits. Information technology enables people to search for a lot of information about the products they like through the Internet. In many countries, online shopping has become an increasingly popular shopping style.

● Sociocultural Environment

The **sociocultural environment** includes institutions and other forces that influence a society's basic values, perceptions, preferences and behaviors. The social conditions in which people grow up shape their belief systems and behaviors for the rest of their lives. Values and attitudes that a person acquired early in life are difficult or even impossible to change, and they affect his or her purchase decisions in many ways. To understand how sociocultural environment affects marketing decisions, marketers have to take into consideration the items as follows.

The core beliefs and values people hold in a given society are hard to change. For example, the Chinese Hui ethnic people do not eat pork. This belief affects their shopping habits since they do not buy anything related to pork. Moreover, core beliefs and values will pass on from parents to children and are reinforced by school, business and government. Marketers have little chance to change core beliefs and values.

In comparison, secondary beliefs and values are easier to change. For example, if some eating habits are not restricted by religious taboos but out of some experience in the past, they are easily changed, thus marketers have some chance to change such secondary values.

Furthermore, successful marketers are able to predict cultural shifts in order to find out new opportunities or threats. For example, in China, with the improvement of standard of living since the last two decades, more people shift their emphasis in life from getting enough food and clothes to physical fitness and well-being. Such information helps marketers cater to trends with appropriate products and communication appeals.

Marketers should also consider people's views towards both people (including themselves and the people around them) and things (such as organizations, nature, the society and the universe). For example, people with different views about themselves will choose products of different brands and price levels. For another instance, in the year 2008, the Chinese people have quite special views towards the Olympics, so that many marketers seized the chance and developed various kinds of products, including things for collection, clothes, food and so on. Products or services bearing the Olympic image have entered almost every corner of the Chinese people's life. People in Beijing, Qingdao and Dalian have enjoyed a great boom in the tourist industry after the 29th Olympics.

● Political Environment

Marketing decisions are strongly affected by the development in the **political environment**. The political environment consists of laws, government agencies and pressure groups that influence and limit various organizations and individuals in a given society.

Business activities need a stable political environment. Thanks to the economic reform and opening up policy, China's economy has been enjoying strong growth driven by the favorable political and economical environment since 1978.

To begin with, the state policy and regulations for business enjoys constant improvement. With the development of marketing economy in China, the government has passed a lot of laws and regulations related to economic development. Business legislation has been enacted for the following purposes.

- To protect the legal interests of enterprises, so as to avoid unfair competition and ensure a fine marketing system.
- To protect consumers from unfair business practices. Unfair business practices have been defined and are monitored by various agencies.
- To protect the interest of the society. Regulations force companies to be responsible for the social costs of their production or products.

Moreover, associations representing public interests have gained rapid development. Nowadays, with consumers' clearer awareness of their legal rights and interests, non-governmental organizations such as consumers associations and environmental protection organizations were founded one after another. These organizations are not enforced by law or the government, but they are generally spokesmen for a certain group of people, so they are influential to some extent. For example, some organizations may guide or prevent the consuming needs of a certain group of consumers, constituting considerable pressure to marketing behaviors and marketing position of a company. In China, the most influential one of this kind is the China Consumers Association, which was established in Beijing in January of 1985. It performs social supervision on the commodity and services so as to protect the legal rights and interests of consumers.

(Adapted from Gary Armstrong & Philip Kotler, *Marketing: An Introduction*, Prentice-Hall, Inc.2000:84; William O., Bearden, et al. *Marketing: Principle & Perspective*, McGraw-Hill, 1998: 64.)

Activity 1

Case 1: Several decades ago, the United States of America once enjoyed the reputation as "the state on the automobile wheel" for its proud advanced automobile industry. But only within a short period of time, the Japanese-made petrol-saving automobiles occupied a large proportion of the American market.

Question: Please search the Internet for the features of American and Japanese automobiles respectively and then discuss the following questions in groups of 3 or 4 according to the information given in the supplementary material.

1. Why the American automobile market was largely occupied by the Japanese cars?
2. Compare the two pictures and tell which car looks younger and is more popular?

Case 2: An American company used the advertising catchword "Do what you want to!" while pushing its new products in the Japanese market, but the event led to an unfavorable result. However, after a careful study of the Japanese society, the company changed the words into "Do what you should do!" And the market improved greatly.

Question: Please search the Internet for some features of American sociocultural values and those of the Japanese, then discuss the following questions in groups.

1. Why did the company achieve quite different results just because of one different word in their slogan?
2. Are these two slogans greatly different from each other?

Activity 2

Suppose you are going to set up a company of your own, you have the following places (as shown in the picture) to choose from. Which one (ones) would you choose, and which one (ones) would you not choose? Discuss in groups of 3 or 4 and state your reasons using the information about the different types of environment that you have learned in the readings.

Picture 1 A crowed shopping center

Picture 2 Affluent residential zones

Picture 3 A stable society

Picture 4 A war-torn society

(Pictures are from http://www.image.baidu.com.)

Activity 3

Translation and Discussion (2)

Translate the following story and the questions into English, and then discuss the questions in English.

为了繁荣经济，创造更多的就业机会，国家鼓励自主创业，并制定了相关的优惠政策和措施。韩柳决定到当地的相关部门了解一下，国家对于大学生创业到底有哪些具体的优惠政策。

问题

1. 你认为韩柳应该到什么部门去了解情况呢？
2. 有哪些政府鼓励创业的优惠政策呢？

 Supplementary Material

Responding to the Marketing Environment

Someone once observed, "Towards the issue of marketing environment, there are three kinds of companies: those who make things happen, those who watch things happen, and those who wonder what's happened."

Many companies view the marketing environment as an uncontrollable element to which they must adapt. They passively accept the marketing and do not try to change it. They analyze the environmental forces and design strategies that will help the company avoid the threats and take advantage of the opportunities the environment provides.

Other companies take the **environmental management perspective**, a management perspective in which the firm takes aggressive actions to affect the publics and forces in its marketing environment rather than simply watch and react to them. Such companies hire lobbyists to influence legislation affecting their industries and stage media events to gain favorable press coverage. They run advertorials (ads expressing editorial points of view) to shape public opinion. They press lawsuits and file complaints with regulators to keep competitors in line, and they form contractual agreements to better control their distribution channels.

Often, companies can find positive ways to overcome seemingly uncontrollable environmental constraints. For example, Cathay Pacific Airlines determined that many travelers were avoiding Hong Kong because of lengthy delays at immigration. Rather than assuming that this was a problem they could not solve, Cathay's senior staff asked the Hong Kong government how to avoid these immigration delays. After lengthy discussions, the airline agreed to make an annual grant-in-aid to the government to hire more immigration inspectors—but these reinforcements would service primarily the Cathay Pacific gates. The reduced waiting period increased customer value and thus strengthened the company's efficiency.

Marketing management cannot always control environmental forces. In many cases, it must settle for simply watching and reacting to the environment. For example, a company would have little success trying to influence geographic population shifts, the economic environment, or major cultural values. But whenever possible, smart marketing managers will take a proactive rather than reactive approach to the marketing environment.

(Adapted from Gary Armstrong & Philip Kotler, *Marketing: An Introduction*, Prentice-Hall Inc. 2000:96.)

Questions

1. How can a real estate company respond to the aged tendency of population?
2. Energy shortage is a worldwide problem. How can a car maker react to this environment?

Unit 3

Marketing Research

After learning this unit, you will be able to answer the following questions.

- How can we write a research report?
- Why do we need to do market research?
- How can a questionnaire be designed?
- How can data be collected?
- What are the steps in market research?

📖 Warm-up Activities

American marketing expert Gilbert A. Churchill, Jr. once said in his book that "Marketing research really began to grow when firms found they could no longer sell all they could produce, but instead had to gauge market needs and produce accordingly."

Pre-reading questions: What do you know about market research? Do you think it is popular in your country? Please give some examples of market research activity that you witness in daily life.

Reading 1

Why Do We Need to Do Market Research?

Juicy Fruit Gum, the oldest brand of the Wm. Wrigley Jr. Company, wasn't chewing up the teen market, gum's top consumer. A few years ago the company found itself under pressure from competitors. Sales and market share were down. How could Wrigley make more young people chew Juicy Fruit? What qualities about Juicy Fruit appeal to teens? Wrigley decided to launch massive market research. From initial marketing research, Wrigley learned that teens chew Juicy Fruit because it's sweet. It refreshes and energizes them. Follow-up research by advertising agency BBDO confirmed what the teens were saying. BBDO asked more than four hundred heavy gum chewers to rate various brands by attributes that best represented them. For Juicy Fruit, respondents picked phrases such as "has the right amount of sweetness" and "is made with natural sweeteners". Clearly the advertising needed to focus on the gum's sweet, satisfying qualities.

Then, BBDO developed four TV commercials with the "Gotta Have Sweet" theme and asked teens to evaluate them. The campaign debuted in late 1998 with an assortment of radio and TV spots geared to twelve-to-twenty-four-year-olds. BBDO also created Juicy Fruit bookcovers to tie into the back-to-school season. One design featured a cheerleader lifting a car to find a pack of Juicy Fruit. Sales of 100-stick boxes of Juicy Fruit rose 5 percent after the start of the ad campaign, versus a 2 percent decline prior to it. Juicy Fruit's market share also increased to 5.3 percent from 4.9 percent, the biggest gain of any established chewing gum brand during the year following the campaign.

Clearly, the series of marketing research studies helped Juicy Fruit raise its market share. The decision makers need information. Different companies need different kinds of information, and the information can be gathered in many different ways. Marketing research is the function that links the consumer, customer and public to the marketer through information. The information has at least the following functions: identify and define marketing opportunities and problems; generate, refine, and evaluate marketing actions; monitor marketing performance; and improve people's understanding of marketing as a process. Sales people use the results of marketing research studies to better sell their products. Politicians use marketing research to plan campaign strategies. Even clergy use marketing research to determine when to hold service. The point is that an essential activity can take many forms, but its basic function is to gather information needed to help managers make better decisions.

(Adapted from Charles W. Lamb, et al., *Marketing*, 6th Edition, South-Western Educational Publishing, 2002, Chapter 8.)

Concept Check

1. Marketing research is the function that _____.
2. The basic function of marketing research is _____.

Oral practice

Describe the market research done by BBDO in your own words.

Group Discussion

Successful sales promotion activities are always conducted after a thorough market research. Have a discussion about whether marketing research is relevant to the following organizations according to their sales campaign that you witness.

- Pepsicola
- Apple
- Huawei
- A local supermarket nearby

 Reading 2

How to Collect Data

For the marketers, market research results in finding problems and opportunities. Data collection can be done in collecting primary data and secondary data. First attempts at data collection should focus on secondary data, which are statistics not gathered for the immediate study at hand but previously gathered for some other purposes. Information originated by the researcher for the purpose of the investigation at hand is called primary data.

Secondary data often include documents such as annual reports, reports to stockholders, product testing results, records, memos, warranty cards and periodicals, etc. The most significant advantages of secondary data are the time and money they save. The researcher can simply go to the library or go on-line, locate the appropriate source or sources, and gather the information desired. This should take no more than a few days and involve little cost. Even if there is a charge for using the data, the cost is still substantially less than that spent by the firm when collecting the information by itself. But secondary data has its unavoidable disadvantages: ① they do not completely fit the problem; ② they are not totally accurate.

In contrast, primary data collecting is usually committed by communication and observation. Communication involves questioning respondents to secure the desired information, by a data collection instrument called a questionnaire. The questions may be oral or in writing, and the responses may also be given in either form. Observation does not involve questioning. Rather, it means that the situation of interest is scrutinized and the relevant facts, actions, or behaviors are recorded. The observer may be one or more persons or a mechanical device. The choice of survey method will depend on several factors. These include the following.

● **Speed:** Email and Web page surveys are the fastest methods, followed by telephone interviewing. Mail surveys are the slowest.

● **Cost:** Personal interviews are the most expensive followed by telephone and then mail. Email and Web page surveys are the least expensive for large samples.

● **Internet Usage:** Web page and Email surveys offer significant advantages, but you may not be able to generalize their results to the population as a whole.

● **Literacy Levels:** Illiterate and less-educated people rarely respond to mail surveys.

● **Sensitive Questions:** People are more likely to answer sensitive questions when interviewed directly by a computer in one form or another.

● **Video, Sound, Graphics:** A need to get reactions to video, music or a picture limits your options. You can play a video on a Web page, in a computer-direct interview, or in person. You can play music when using these methods or over a telephone. You can show pictures in those first methods and in a mail surveys.

It is one thing to figure out with whom to make contact in research; it is quite another to get them to agree to participate. In this respect, the personal interview affords the most sample control. With a personal interview, the respondent's identity is known; thus there is little opportunity for anyone else to reply. While interviews by telephone, e-mail or web-administered questionnaires are popular when the respondents are far away, they may result in refusals to participate.

(Adapted from http://www. surveysystem. com/sdesign. htm#design.)

Concept Check

1. Secondary data refer to _____.

2. Primary data refer to _____.

3. Secondary data often include _____.

4. The advantages of secondary data are _____, while the disadvantages are _____.

5. In contrast, primary data collecting is usually committed by _____.

 **Activity 1**

What Are the Steps of A Market Research?

The functions of market research can be planning, problem solving and controlling. Exhibit 3.1 can illustrate what questions marketers should address in a market research.

Ⅰ.Planning

1. Who would buy our products? Where do they live? How are their incomes? What is the number of our customer?

2. Are the markets for our products expanding or shrinking? Are there any potential markets that we have not yet reached?

3. Are the channels of distribution for our products changing? Are there any new type of marketing institutions evolving?

Ⅱ.Problem solving

A. Product

1. Which of the various product designs is likely to be the most successful?

2. What kind of packaging should we use?

B. Price

1. What price should we charge for our products?

2. As production costs decline, should we lower our prices or try to develop higher-quality products?

C. Place

1. Where and by whom, should our products be sold?

2. What kinds of incentives should we offer the trader to push our products?

D. Promotion

1. How much should we spend on promotion? How should it be allocated to products and to geographic areas?

> 2. What combination of media—newspapers, radio, television, magazines, the Internet—should we use?
>
> Ⅲ .Control
>
> 1. What is our market share overall? In each geographic area? By each customer type?
>
> 2. Are customers satisfied with our products? How is our record for service? Are there many returns?
>
> 3. How does the public perceive our company? What is our reputation with the trade?

Exhibit 3.1 Kinds of Questions Marketing Research Can Help Answer

No matter what the cost of a market research project is, the same general process should be as follows: ① identifying and formulating the problem/opportunity; ② planning the research design and gathering primary data; ③ specifying the sampling procedures; ④ collecting the data; ⑤ analyzing the data; ⑥ preparing and presenting the report; ⑦ following up. Figure 3.1 illustrates the general process of a market research project.

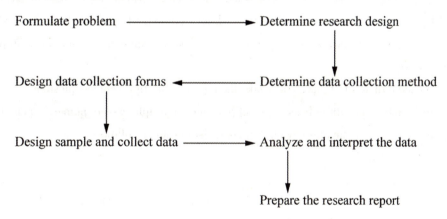

Process of A Market Research Project

Group Discussion

After studying the above Exhibit and figure carefully, discuss with your group members and try to find possible answers to the following cases.

1. An American manufacturer of cornflakes tries to introduce its product to China, but the company knows little about the Chinese market, what could the manufacturer do to know more about the Chinese market? How could they do it?

2. Mr. Hu wants to set up a supermarket near a university. What should he do before starting the business?

 **Activity 2**

How to Design a Questionnaire

The Steps Required to Design and Administer A Questionnaire

1. Defining the Objectives of the Survey
2. Determining the Sampling Group
3. Writing the Questionnaire
4. Administering the Questionnaire
5. Interpretation of the Results

Question Types

In general, there are two types of questions one will ask: open format or closed format.

Open format questions are those that ask for unprompted opinions. In other words, there is no predetermined set of responses, and the participant is free to answer whatever they choose.

Closed format questions usually take the form of a multiple-choice question.

Researchers use three basic types of questions: multiple choice, numeric open end and text open end. Examples of each kind of questions are as follows.

Multiple Choice

1. Where do you live?
   A. North   B. South   C. East   D. West

Numeric Open End

2. How much did you spend on groceries this week?
   _____

Text Open End

3. How can our company improve its working conditions?
   _____
   _____

Rating Scales and Agreement Scales are two common types of questions that some researchers treat as multiple choice questions and others treat as numeric open end questions. Examples of these kinds of questions are as follows.

Rating Scales

4. How would you rate this product?

☐ Excellent
☐ Good
☐ Fair
☐ Poor

5. On a scale where "10" means you have a great amount of interest in a subject and "1" means you have none at all, how would you rate your interest in each of the following topics?

Domestic politics .. —
Foreign Affairs ...... —
Science & Health .. —
Business .... —

Agreement Scale

6. How much do you agree with each of the following statements:

	Strongly Agree	Agree	Disagree	Strongly Disagree
My manager provides constructive criticism.	☐	☐	☐	☐
Our medical plan provides adequate coverage.	☐	☐	☐	☐
I would prefer to work longer hours on fewer days.	☐	☐	☐	☐

General Consideration

- The first rule is keeping it short and simple.
- If necessary, place the questions into three groups: must know, useful to know and nice to know.
- Start with an introduction or welcome message.
- Allow a "Don't Know" or "Not Applicable" response to all questions.
- For the same reason, include "Other" or "None".

Tips

You may want to leave a space for the respondent to add their name and title.

Do not put two questions into one. Avoid questions such as "Do you buy frozen meat and frozen fish?"

Avoid emotionally charged words or leading questions that point towards a certain answer.

Avoid technical terms and acronyms, unless you are absolutely sure that respondents know what they mean.

Make sure your questions accept all the possible answers. A question like "Do you go to school by car or by bike?" does not cover all possible answers.

(Adapted from http://www.surveysystem.com/sdesign.htm#design.)

Activity 1

Look at the following layouts of questions and decide which you would prefer to use. Why?

(1) Do you agree, disagree or have no opinion that this company has

A good vacation policy — agree/not sure/disagree

Good management feedback — agree/not sure/disagree

Good medical insurance — agree/not sure/disagree

High wages — agree/not sure/disagree

An alternative layout is as follows.

(2) Do you agree, disagree or have no opinion that this company has

	Agree	Not sure	Disagree
A good vacation policy	☐ 1	☐ 2	☐ 3
Good management feedback	☐ 1	☐ 2	☐ 3
Good medical insurance	☐ 1	☐ 2	☐ 3
High wages	☐ 1	☐ 2	☐ 3

Activity 2

You go shopping in two groceries or supermarkets nearby to do the following market research. The objective is to assess the check-out service provided to customers. You would complete the following table.

(1) Store Name _____ Date _____

  Location _____ Time _____

(2) Observation

Long wait in line at the check-out	Yes	No
Cashier: quick and efficient	Yes	No
Cashier: prices well recorded	Yes	No

Cashier: friendly and pleasant	Yes	No
Purchases packed quickly	Yes	No
Purchases packed poorly	Yes	No
Trolley provided	Yes	No
Bags provided were flimsy	Yes	No
Bags provided were attractive	Yes	No
Other facts _____		

Compare the two sets of results and discuss the strengths and weaknesses of different stores.

 ## Activity 3

Translation and Discussion (3)

Translate the following story and the questions into English, and then discuss the questions in English.

经过一番争论，三人决定做服装生意。他们首先想到的是在市中心的服装城租个门面卖服装。服装生意利润不错，但竞争相当激烈，到底卖什么服装好呢？学市场营销的韩柳马上想到的是：他们应该先做一个市场调查。

问题
1. 你认为他们的市场调查应该调查什么？
2. 他们可以采取什么方法来调查？

How to Write a Good Research Report

After you have done your Market Research work, you have to write a report. However, the best research can put aside without being read. Following are a few tips for writing a good Market Research Report that you can be proud of.

The first thing you have to do is to get your reader's attention with a powerful headline and a good opening summary. If you fail to get your prospect's attention, you will fail to communicate and deliver the benefits of your research.

Always remember that if your report is not read and action taken, your company will receive no benefits from all the research that you have done, and that's a pretty damn shame. But if you do the report right, you are probably about 70 percent of the way to a promotion. So read on and pay attention.

The trick is writing a research report that will grab the reader's attention without allowing his or her mind to wander even for a second. Or worse: making a copy mistake that turns her or him off entirely—and gets your research report instantly tossed into the nearest virtual or literal trash can.

In a very real sense, your body copy is a minefield that must be navigated with the greatest of care: Every word, every sentence and paragraph of body copy represents the chance to either intensify your prospect's focus ... or to completely lose him.

The following seven rules can help you produce a top quality Market Research Report.

Rule 1: Keep Your Report Logically Organized

Humans are NOT logical animals. But when reading or learning, they generally require that the material be presented in a clear, logical way. That generally means starting at point "A" ... progressing to point "B" ... moving on to point "C" ... and so on, until you have reached your ultimate conclusion.

To do that, you must build your case logically and methodically—much like a mason builds a brick wall. You must lay a solid foundation of research and then build upon each completed analysis argument with the next ... brick by brick ... in a logical order, proving your research points.

Ask yourself, "What must my reader know first ... second ... third ... and so on, in order to conclude that this research offers the opportunity of a lifetime?"

Rule 2: Keep the Report Moving

When a reader's eyes first fall upon your report, a little stopwatch starts ticking in his head. If at any point, he feels you're not moving along quickly enough, you will lose him.

Creating a dynamic flow of information in your research report is absolutely essential for maximum readability. There are three ways to do it.

a) Creating and following a "chain of logic" outline helps a lot in this regard—by ensuring that you make each point once, then move on. If prospects feel like you're going back over stuff you already covered, any sense of momentum you may have established is instantly destroyed.

b) Check the momentum of each draft by reading it aloud. Mark the places where you—as a reader—begin to become distracted or bored. Once again, highlight any sections that begin to lose you. Each of these sections will kill readership and response if they're still there in the final draft. Edit them or delete them.

c) Making each section of copy shorter than the one before is a great way to create momentum. For example—let's say you have to make ten analysis points in order to complete the report. You could spend one and half pages making your first analysis, one page making your second, 3/4 of a page making your third, 1/2 page making your fourth, and then wrap up the final six points in a series of bullets covering a single page.

Rule 3: Keep Your Report Simple

Never ask your prospect to work in order to figure out what you're saying. Two-dollar words, esoteric references and complex sentences are killers in research reports. Subtlety, nuance and complexity are for poets—NOT market reports!

Try to limit yourself to one complete, clearly presented thought per sentence. When you connect two thoughts in a sentence, make sure they connect directly and clearly with each other. Also be sure to avoid inserting undeveloped or underdeveloped thoughts in sentences or paragraphs.

Rule 4: Keep the Report Fat-Free

Readers should feel as though they're getting good value in return for the number of words they're made to read. Your challenge is to never use three words when two will do the job. Here are four ways to say more with less.

a) Use more precise word choices: When you fail to use the word that most precisely and accurately communicates a thought, you wind up using five, six or even ten words instead. When searching for the most precise word, checking synonyms in a thesaurus often gives you the answer.

b) Eliminate unnecessary words: Here again, reading copy aloud really helps. Much of the time, for example, the word "that" is totally unnecessary. When in doubt, leave it out!

c) Avoid unhelpful repetition: Repetition of key sales points or major benefits is a beautiful thing. Repeating minor thoughts only slows the copy and bores the reader.

d) Figures of speech can help you say more, faster: If a picture is worth a thousand words, metaphors, similes, and other figures of speech are as well.

Rule 5: Keep Your Report Believable

Your reader is already skeptical. Making grandiose claims that you can't (or don't) prove beyond the shadow of a doubt will only confirm what he or she already suspects: that you're full of beans. And this will get your promotion trashed in a heartbeat.

Rule 6: Keep Your Report Potent

One of the fastest ways to lose your prospect's attention is to fail to focus on his favorite subject: HIM or HER! The word "You" has been called the most powerful word in the English language—and for good reason. Finding ways to personalize the report—applying each passage as if had been written for the reader—is a key to keeping his attention.

Rule 7: Avoid Unintended Impressions

Here's where insisting that friends read your report can pay huge dividends. By the time you're ready to stick a fork in your new promotion, you can almost recite it word for word—forwards and backwards. That means you're too close to the report to catch things that may be misread, even things that may raise objections or implant an erroneous impression in your reader's mind.

Bottom line: Your research report is only as strong as its weakest link. And that makes it essential to get downright obsessive about every word, every turn of phrase, every jot and title. Yes, it takes work. But do it right, and the rewards can be truly spectacular.

(Adapted from www.allabout marketresearch. com)

Application

Conduct market research on the college students' using of cellphones in your school, and write a report.

Unit 4

Target Market

After learning this unit, you will be able to answer the following questions.

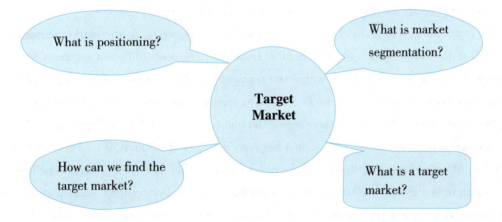

Warm-up

P&G company has developed different kinds of toothpaste under the brand crest(佳洁士). How many types of products can you list? How are they different from each other? Work with your group members and complete the following table.

Toothpaste	For what kind of people?
Crest （草本）	For those who are price sensitive and pursue natural flavor
Crest （炫白）	
Crest （盐白）	
Crest （茶爽）	
…	

 Reading 1

What Is Market Segmentation?

The marketing concept calls for understanding customers and satisfying their needs better than competitors. Markets consist of buyers, and buyers differ in one or more ways. They may differ in their wants, resources, locations, buying attitudes and buying practices, and it is rarely possible to satisfy all customers by treating them alike. Market segmentation is a strategy that involves dividing a larger market into subsets of consumers who have common needs and applications for the goods and services offered in the market. Through market segmentation, companies can reach customers more efficiently and effectively with products and services that match customers' unique needs.

In other words, the aim of segmenting a market is to allow the marketing program to focus on the subset of prospects that are "most likely" to purchase the offerings. If done properly, this will help to insure the highest return for a company's marketing expenditures.

By segmenting, a large market is divided into several *segments*. A true market segment meets all of the following criteria: it is distinct from other segments (different segments have different needs); it is homogeneous within the segment (exhibits common needs); it responds similarly to a market stimulus, and it can be reached by communication and distribution channels.

Segments can be identified in three ways. The traditional approach is to divide the market into *demographic groups*, such as "women between the ages of 35 and 50". This has the advantage of ease of reaching this group. Its disadvantage is that there is no reason to believe that women in this group have similar needs or readiness to buy. Demographic segmentation is more about identifying a population *sector* than a population *segment*. The second approach is to segment the market into *need groups*, such as "women who want to save time in shopping for food". This is a clear need that can be met by a number of solutions, such as a supermarket taking telephone orders or Web orders that would be delivered to the home. The hope would be to identify demographic or psychographic characteristics of such women, such as being more highly educated or having a higher income. The third approach is to segment the market by *behavior groups*, such as "women who order their food from Peapod and other home delivery groups". This group is defined by their actual behavior, not just needs, and the analyst can then search for common characteristics that they may have. Once you identify a distinct segment, the question is whether it should be managed within the existing organization or deserves to be set up as a separate business. In other words, are you going to choose this segment as your target market?

(Adapted from Philip Kotler, *Marketing Insights from A to Z-80 Concepts Every Manager Needs to Know*, John Wiley & Sons, Inc., P.163.)

Question

How will you group your classmates according to their eating behaviour?

Reading 2

Market Targeting

Market segmentation divides the market into several segments. The one or ones that you choose to serve is called your target market(s). The term target market is used because that market is the target at which you aim all your marketing efforts.

Targeting is a process of decision making. Among the segments, the firm has to evaluate each segment and decide how many and which ones to target. In evaluating different market segments, a firm must look at two dimensions: segment attractiveness and company fit.

The company must first collect and analyze data on current sales value, projected sales-growth rates and expected profit margins for the various segments. Segments with the right size and growth characteristics are interesting. But "right size and growth" are relative matters. Some companies will want to target segments with large current sales, a high growth rate and a high profit margin. However, the largest, fastest-growing segments are not always the most attractive ones for every company. Smaller companies may find that they lack the skills and resources needed to serve the larger segments, or that these segments are too competitive. Such companies may select segments that are smaller and less attractive, in an absolute sense, but that are potentially more profitable for them. A segment might have desirable size and growth and still not be attractive from a profitability point of view. The company must examine several significant structural factors that affect long-run segment attractiveness. For example, the company should assess current and potential competitors. A segment is less attractive if it already contains many strong and aggressive competitors. Marketers also should consider the threat of substitute products. A segment is less attractive if actual or potential substitutes for the product already exist. Substitutes limit the potential prices and profits from segments. The relative power of buyers also affects segment attractiveness. If the buyers in a segment possess strong or increasing bargaining power relative to sellers, they will try to force prices down, demand more quality or services, and set competitors against one another. All these actions will reduce the sellers' profitability. Finally, segment attractiveness depends on the relative power of suppliers. A segment is less attractive if the suppliers of raw materials, equipment, labor and services in the segment are powerful enough to raise prices or reduce the duality or quantity of ordered goods and services. Suppliers tend to be powerful when they are large and concentrated, when few substitutes exist, or when the supplied product is an important input.

When a segment is attractive enough, the company must then decide whether it has the skills and resources needed to succeed in that segment. Each segment has certain success requirements. If the company lacks and cannot readily obtain the strengths needed to compete successfully in a segment, it should not enter the segment. Even if the company possesses the required strengths, it needs to employ skills to find resources superior to those of the competition to really win in a market segment. The company should enter segments only where it can offer superior value and gain advantages over competitors.

(Adapted from Philip Kotler, et al., *Principles of Marketing*, Pearson Education Australia, 2006, pp. 229–230.)

Question

How can a company decide that a segment is attractive to it?

Understanding Positioning

A product's position is the way the product is defined by consumers on important attributes—the place the product occupies in consumers' minds relative to competing products.

Choose the words below that you think well describe the image of the product in your mind (you can choose only one alternative for each item).

1. luxury   2. good performance   3. high technology   4. economy

1. anti-scurf   2. refreshing   3. moisturizing   4. softening

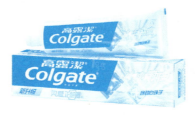

1. whitening your teeth   2. strengthening your teeth   3. cheap   4. fresh

1. comfortable   2. professional   3. economy   4. durable

Now think about the question. How did you get these kinds of impressions on the products above? Tell your answers to your classmates.

(Pictures are from http://image.baidu.com.)

Activity 2

Positioning Strategy

Consumers position products with or without the help of marketers. But marketers do not want to leave their products' positions to chance. They must plan positions that will give their products the greatest advantage in selected target markets, and they must design marketing mixes to create these planned positions.

Application

Please go to the Internet or other resources to find out the most influencing advertisements for the following products.

Products	Advertisements	Images created
	我的地盘 听我的	

Activity 3

Translation and Discussion (4)

Translate the following story and the questions into English, and then discuss the questions in English.

经过调查，韩柳等人发现本地的服装店主要分为女装店、男装店、童装店和男女混装店（即既卖男装又卖女装的店，目标客户主要为16～26岁左右的青年男女）。女装店主要经营青春少女装，适合35～45岁白领女性的服装很少。经过认真思考，他们决定选择35～45岁左右的职业女性作为目标市场。

问题

1. 他们这样选择的合理性在哪里？有可能面临怎样的挑战？
2. 你知道哪些做职业女装的品牌？他们是如何定位的？

Supplementary Material

Positioning

Thanks to Al Ries and Jack Trout, "positioning" entered the marketing vocabulary in 1982 when they wrote Positioning: The Battle for Your Mind. Actually the word had been used earlier in connection with placing products in stores, hopefully at the eye-level position. However, Ries and Trout gave a new twist to the term: "But positioning is not what you do to a product. Positioning is what you do to the mind of the prospect." Thus Volvo tells us that it makes "the safest car" ; BMW is "the ultimate driving machine" ; and Porsche is "the world's best small sports car."

A company can claim to be different from and better than another company in numerous ways: We are faster, safer, cheaper, more convenient, more durable, more friendly, higher quality, better value..., the list goes on. But Ries and Trout emphasized the need to choose one of these so that it would stick in the buyer's mind. They saw positioning as primarily a communication exercise. Unless a product is identified as being best in some way that is meaningful to some set of customers, it will be poorly positioned and poorly remembered. We remember brands that stand out as first or best in some way.

But the positioning cannot be arbitrary. We wouldn't be able to get people to believe that Hyundai is "the ultimate driving machine" . In fact, the product must be designed with an intended positioning in mind; the positioning must be decided before the product is designed. One of the tragic flaws in General Motors' car lineup is that it designs cars without distinctive positioning. After the car is made, GM struggles to decide how to position it.

Brands that are not number one in their market (measured by company size or some other attribute) don't have to worry—they simply need to select another attribute and be number one on that attribute. I consulted with a drug company that positioned its new drug as "fastest in relief" . Its new competitor then positioned its brand as "safest" . Each competitor will attract those customers who favor its major attribute.

Some companies prefer to build a multiple positioning instead of just a single positioning. The drug company could have called its drug the "fastest and safest drug on the market" . But then another new competitor could co-opt the position "least expensive" . Obviously, if a company claims too many superior attributes it won't be remembered or believed. Occasionally, however, this works, as when the toothpaste Aquafresh claimed that it offered a three-in-one benefit: fights cavities, whitens teeth, and gives cleaner breath.

Michael Treacy and Fred Wiersema distinguished among three major positionings (which they called "value disciplines"): product leadership, operational excellence, and customer intimacy. Some customers value most the firm that offers the best product in the category; others value the firm that operates most efficiently; and still others value the firm that responds best to their wishes. They advise a firm to become the acknowledged leader in one of these value disciplines and be at least adequate in the other two. It would be too difficult or expensive for a company to be best in all three value disciplines.

Recently Fred Crawford and Ryan Mathews suggested five possible positionings: product, price, ease of access, value-added service, and customer experience. Based on their study of successful companies, they concluded that a great company will dominate on one of these, perform above the average (differentiate) on a second, and be at industry par with respect to the remaining three. As an example, Wal-Mart dominates on price, differentiates on product (given its huge variety), and is average at ease of access, value added service, and the customer experience. Crawford and Mathews hold that a company will suboptimize if it tries to be best in more than two ways.

The most successful positioning occurs with companies that have figured out how to be unique and very difficult to imitate. No one has successfully copied IKEA, Harley Davidson, Southwest Airlines, or Neutragena. These companies have developed hundreds of special processes for running their businesses. Their outer shells can be copied but not their inner workings.

Companies that lack a unique positioning can sometimes make a mark by resorting to the "number two" strategy. Avis is remembered for its motto: "We're number two. We try harder." And 7-Up is remembered for its "Uncola" strategy.

Alternatively, a company can claim to belong to the exclusive club of the top performers in its industry: the Big Three auto firms, the Big Five accounting firms. They exploit the aura of being in the leadership circle that offers higher-quality products and services than those on the outside.

No positioning will work forever. As changes occur in consumers, competitors, technology, and the economy, companies must reevaluate the positioning of their major brands. Some brands that are losing share may need to be repositioned. This must be done carefully. Remaking your brand may win new customers but lose some current customers who like the brand as it is. If Volvo, for example, placed less emphasis on safety and more on slick styling, this could turn off practical-minded Volvo fans.

(Philip Kotler, *Marketing Insights from A to Z-80 Concepts Every Manager Needs to Know*, John Wiley & Sons, Inc., pp.135-138.)

Questions

1. How do you understand the phrase "positioning is a communication process"?

2. "Wong Lo Kat" (王老吉) was originally a brand of herbal tea (凉茶). Herbal tea is only popular in Guangdong province and the southern part of Guangxi. People in other parts of China think herbal tea is a kind of medicine and very bitter, and will not buy it as a drink. However, the manufacturer JDB Group successfully repositioned herbal tea and has sold it to most parts of China. Find out the repositioning story of the product and share it with your classmates.

Unit 5

New Product Development

After learning this unit, you will be able to answer the following questions.

- How can a new product be launched?
- What is called a new product?
- New Product
- How can we come up with new product ideas?
- What are the steps of developing a new product?

Warm-up

Once an organization loses its spirit of pioneering and rests on its early work, its progress stops.

— Thomas Watson, the American President of IBM (International Business Machine) from 1920s to 1950s.

What's your understanding of the above quote? How important do you think innovation is to a business?

Reading 1

What Is A New Product?

New products are important to sustain growth and profits and to replace obsolete items. **3M Corp**. introduces about 500 new products each year. Johnson & Johnson and Gillette expect products launched in the past five years to account for 36 and 50 percent of annual revenue, respectively.

The number of new product introductions continues to rise. However, Less than 6 percent of the new products introduced in most years appear to be truly innovative.

The term new product is somewhat confusing, because its meaning varies widely. Actually, there are several "correct" definitions of the term. A product can be new to the world, to the market, to the producer or seller, or to some combination of these. There are six categories of new products.

New-to-the-world products (also called discontinuous innovations): These products create an entirely new market. The telephone, television, computer, and facsimile machine are commonly cited examples of new-to-the-world products.

New product lines: These products, which the firm has not previously offered, allow it to enter an established market. Heinz Frozen Foods recently introduced a new product line called Boston Market Home Style following a ten-year licensing deal with Boston Chicken, Inc.. The new line will anchor the premium end of three Heinz lines that include Budget Gourmet (a value product line) and Smart Ones (a nutritionally oriented product line).

Additions to existing product lines: This category includes new products that supplement a firm's established line. Gillette's MACH 3 is an addition to the company's blades and razors product line.

Improvement and revisions of existing products: The "new and improved" product may be significantly or slightly changed. For example, Breyers ice cream "scoops right out without bending the spoon". Anyone who has ever sat around for fifteen minutes waiting for a half-gallon of ice cream to thaw would certainly agree that this is a product improvement. Most new products fit into this category.

Repositioned products: These are existing products targeted at new markets or market segments. Following a 2 to 3 percent annual sales decline for ten years, Cutty Sark Scots Whiskey is no longer trying to compete head-on with super premium brands like Glenfiddich and blended Scotch brands such as Chivas Regal and Dewars. The new target is twenty-something blue-collar males.

Lower-priced products: This category refers to products that provide performance similar to competing brands at a lower price. Hewlett-Packard (HP) Laser Jet 3100 is a scanner, copier, printer and fax machine combined. This new product is priced lower than many conventional color copiers and much lower than the combined price of the four items purchased separately.

These different categories are displayed in the following diagram.

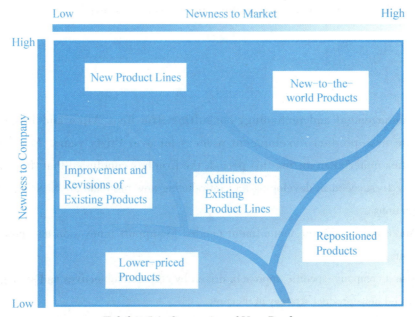

Exhibit 5.1 Categories of New Products

(Adapted from Charles W. Lamb, et al., *Marketing*, 6th Edition, South-Western Educational Publishing, 2002, Chapter 10.)

Notes

① 3M Corp.: 3M is fundamentally a science-based company in the United States. It produces thousands of imaginative products, and it's a leader in scores of markets—from health care and highway safety to office products and optical films for LCD displays. (See more information at http://www.3m.com)

② Heinz: 亨氏

③ Product line: Group of products manufactured by a firm that are closely related in use and in production and marketing requirements. The depth of the product line refers to the number of different products offered in a product line. For example, General Foods has about a dozen different products in its coffee product line. Each of these items is promoted as distinctive, although they share the same distribution channels and similar manufacturing facilities.

④ Gillette's MACH 3：吉列锋速3

⑤ Breyers ice cream：布鲁尔斯冰淇淋（2012年美国最受欢迎冰淇淋品牌排行榜第三名）

⑥ Glenfiddich：格兰菲迪威士忌

⑦ Chivas Regal：芝华士苏格兰威士忌

⑧ Dewars：帝王威士忌

Application

What are the characteristics of new products?

Can you list some new products that fit into the six categories mentioned above?

Reading 2

The New Product Development Process

The management and technology consulting firm Booz Allen and Hamilton has studied the new-product development process for over thirty years. Analyzing five major studies undertaken during this period, the firm has concluded that the companies most likely to succeed in developing and introducing new products are those that take the following actions.

● Make the long-term commitment needed to support innovation and new product development;

● Use a company-specific approach, driven by corporate objectives and strategies, with a well-defined new-product strategy at its core;

● Capitalize on experience to achieve and maintain competitive advantage;

● Establish an environment—a management style, organizational structure, and degree of top-management support—conducive to achieving company-specific new-product and corporate objectives.

Most companies follow a formal new-product development process, usually starting with a new-product strategy. Exhibit 5.2 traces the seven-step process.

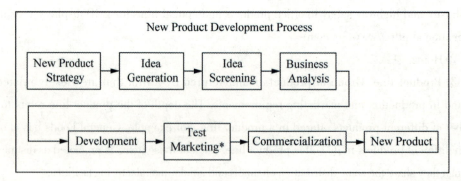

Exhibit 5.2 New-product Development Process

New-product strategy

A new-product strategy is part of the organization's overall marketing strategy. It sharpens the focus and provides general guidelines for generating, screening and evaluating new-product ideas. The new-product strategy specifies the roles that new products must play in the organization's overall plan and describes the characteristics of products the organization wants to offer and the markets it wants to serve.

Idea generation

New-product ideas come from many sources, such as customers, employees, distributors, competitors, research and development, and consultants.

Creativity is the wellspring of new-product ideas, regardless of who comes up with them. A variety of approaches and techniques have been developed to stimulate creative thinking. The two considered most useful for generating new-product ideas are brainstorming and focus group exercised. The goal of brainstorming is to get a group to think of unlimited ways to vary a product or solve a problem. Group members avoid criticism of an idea, no matter how ridiculous it may seem. Objective evaluation is postponed. The sheer quantity of ideas is what matters. An objective of focus group interviews is to stimulate insightful comments through group interaction. Focus groups usually consist of seven to ten people.

Idea screening

After new ideas have been generated, they pass through the first filter in the product development process. This stage, called screening, eliminates ideas that are inconsistent with the organization's new-product strategy or are obviously inappropriate for some other reason. The new-product committee, the new-product department, or some other formally appointed group performs the screening review. At Royal Dutch/Shell, small groups known as "Game Changers" meet weekly online to evaluate new products and process ideas submitted by employees.

Business analysis

New-product ideas that survive the initial screening process move to the business analysis stage, where preliminary figures for demand, cost, sales, and profitability are calculated. For the first time, costs and revenues are estimated and compared. Depending on the nature of the product and the company, this process may be simple or complex.

The newness of the product, the size of the market, and the nature of competition all affect the accuracy of revenue projections. In an established market like soft drinks, industry estimates of total market size are available. Forecasting market share for a new entry is a bigger challenge.

Analyzing overall economic trends and their impact on estimated sales is especially important in product categories that are sensitive to fluctuations in the business cycle. If consumers view the economy as uncertain and risky, they will put off buying durable goods like major home appliances, automobiles, and homes. Likewise, business buyers postponed major equipment purchases if they expect a recession.

Development

In the early stage of development, the R&D department of the engineering department may develop a prototype of the product. During this stage, the firm should start sketching a marketing strategy. The marketing department should decide on the product's packaging, branding, labeling, and so forth. In addition, it should map out preliminary promotion, price, and distribution strategies. The technical feasibility of manufacturing the product at an acceptable cost should also be thoroughly examined.

The development stage can last a long time and thus be very expensive. Crest toothpaste was in the development stage for ten years. It took eighteen years to develop Minute Rice, fifteen years to develop the Polaroid Colorpack camera, fifteen years to develop the Xerox copy machine, and fifty-five years to develop television. Gillette spent six years and more than $750 million developing the MACH 3 razor. Preliminary efforts to develop a three-bladed razor began 28 years before the 1998 launch of MACH 3.

Test marketing

After products and marketing programs have been developed, they are usually tested in the marketplace. Test marketing is the limited introduction of a product and a marketing program to determine the reactions of potential customers in a market situation. Test marketing allows management to evaluate alternative strategies and to assess how well the various aspects of the marketing mix fit together.

Commercialization

The final stage in the new-product development process is commercialization, the decision to market a product. The decision to commercialize the product sets several tasks in motion: ordering production materials and equipment, starting production, building inventories, shipping the product to field distribution points, training the sales force, announcing the new product to the trade, and advertising to potential customers.

The most important factor in successful new-product introduction is a good match between the product and market needs—as the marketing concept would predict. Successful new products deliver a meaningful and perceivable benefit to a suitable number of people or organizations and are different in some meaningful way from their intended substitutes.

(Adapted from Charles W. Lamb, et al., *Marketing*, 6th Edition, South-Western Educational Publishing, 2002, Chapter 10.)

Discussion

1. Explain the importance of an organized new-product development process and illustrate how it might be used for a new hair care product, a new children's toy, and a new mobile phone.

2. Discuss how you might use the new-product development process if you were thinking about offering some kind of summer service to residents in a beach resort town.

3. Try to find one new product development story and share it with your classmates. Suggested story could be about Barbie, Apple, or Wahaha.

 **Activity 1**

How to Come up with New Product Ideas?

Have you ever wanted to add new products to your existing product line? Obviously one way to do that is to find a product that is already developed and start selling that. Another thing you can do is to develop your own new product. Below are 10 ways you can come up with new product ideas.

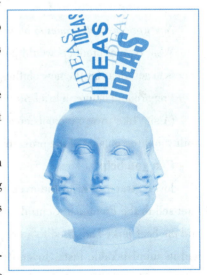

1. Solve an existing problem for people. There are thousands of problems in the world. Create a product that can provide a solution to one of those problems.

2. Find out what's the current hot trend. You can find out what the new trends are by watching TV, reading magazines and surfing the net. Just create a product that's related to the current hot trend.

3. Improve a product that is already on the market. You see products at home, in ads, at stores, etc. Just take a product that's already out there and improve it.

4. Create a new niche for a current product. You can set yourself apart from your competition by creating a niche. Your product could be faster, bigger, smaller, or quicker than your competitor's product.

5. Add on to an existing product. You could package your current product with other

related products. For example, you could package a football with a team jersey and football cards.

6. Reincarnate an older product. Maybe you have a book that's out of print and is no longer being sold. You could change the title, design a new front cover, and bring some of the old content up to date.

7. Ask your current customers. You could contact some of your existing customers by phone or E-mail and ask them what kind of new products they would like to see on the market.

8. Combine two or more products together to create a new one. For example, you could take a brief case and add a thermos compartment inside to keep a drink hot or cold.

9. Survey the people who visit your web site. You could post a survey or questionnaire on your web site. Ask visitors what kind of products they would like to see on the market.

10. You could create a new market for your existing product. For example, if you're selling plastic bottles to a pop company, you could turn around and sell those bottles to a fruit drink company.

Hopefully these 10 ways will get your mind thinking of ways to come up with new product ideas. There is profit to be made for the business who wants to be different and create a new product.

Questions and discussion

Now work in small groups to brainstorm ideas for a new wet-weather clothing line.

What type of products would potential customers want and need? What resources can you access to get ideas for the new clothing line?

Prepare and deliver a brief presentation to your class.

(A site like www.mindtools.com has some great thinking resources for you to improve your ability to think outside of the proverbial box.)

Can you help?

Joyce Strand went to the oven to remove the newest batch of beef jerky that she would later sell to the Frontenac Central Store. To her surprise, she had turned the oven up too high, and the beef jerky had dried to a crisp. Although the texture was much different, the jerky still had its unmistakable taste. Joyce decided to take it to the Central Store anyway and let the customers decide. The new snack became a huge success in the snack food section of the store. Because of her recent success, Joyce began experimenting with different tastes and textures of snack foods that she sells at the Central Store. Realizing that innovation can be very profitable, Joyce now actively looks for new ways to please her customers.

Questions

1. How might Joyce ensure that proper attention is paid to developing new products?

2. What factors should she be aware of that might lead to product failure?

 **Activity 2**

How to Launch a New Product?

The launch of a new product is often an indicator of its future success. Investors, executives and employees want to see the time and money spent in research and development pay off, so you need to strive for a successful product debut.

Prepare for a Successful Product Launch

Step 1

Start advertising the new product several weeks to a month before its launch. Depending on your target market, you may only need to alert your current customers to have a successful debut. Some items, like children's toys, should only be advertised once they are in stores so consumers can buy them shortly after seeing an ad.

Step 2

Coordinate press releases to create a buzz in local and regional media. Journalists love quirky stories, so think about the news value of your product or company. For example, maybe you are the only security-scanner company in the area or are releasing a product that uses a very new technology.

Step 3

Analyze the expected demand of your product so you don't over- or under-shoot your initial product run. Account for sales based on returning customers, media attention and advertising. With some new products, it is often beneficial to inform the public of how many units will be available at launch.

Step 4

Hold a press conference to announce your new product and its release date. This marketing trick requires your product to create such a buzz that consumers and the media talk about it until the launch.

Step 5

Create a website where the curious consumer can learn all about your product. The Internet can be a great place to post deep product specifications that look and feel out of place in an advertisement. Also, include an area where potential customers can post questions about the item.

Step 6

Send out demo units of high-tech gadgets to large newspapers and trade magazines. A review will not only give you some free publicity, you'll also get some general feedback about problems that you may want to correct prior to the launch.

Discussion

Suppose you invented a natural juice that your customers line up to purchase everyday. You have been told too many times that this product should be on supermarket shelves. You have finally decided to do this by having the product tested at a lab for the nutritional facts. However, you are stuck as far as a bottling company goes. Once that is done, **how do you launch this product?** You would like to see it on local supermarket shelves and definitely in schools.

Suggested Answer

To launch a new product you should start by making sure you truly understand who the key target customers are, what their real needs are, why they would buy your product vs. the competition's (what are the strengths & weaknesses of your features and benefits?) and how much they would be willing to pay. You can also conduct market research on your branding and messaging to make sure your product is compelling and distinctive in the market. You should then build your website so people can find you and know you are real. You'll need to decide how you want to market and promote your product—via advertising, PR, online, etc. Remember, you only get one chance to make a great first impression so do your homework for a successful launch.

Activity 3

Translation and Discussion (5)

Translate the following story and the questions into English, and then discuss the questions in English.

开始的时候韩柳等人主要到东莞的服装批发城进货，款式的选择主要依据他们对市场的判断，服装的品牌不固定。开朗的优势在于她对服装的搭配特别有感觉。几个不同牌子的服装，经过她一搭配，总能成套地顺利卖出。在跟顾客的交谈之中她发现，其实这些职业女性心中都有一套自己想要的服装，如果你能够帮助他们实现梦想，找到合适的搭配，那么生意是不用愁了。不过很多时候，开朗发现，顾客的很多要求现成的服装无法满足，于是她萌生了自己设计服装、创自己品牌的想法。

问题

1. 如果开朗真要自己设计服装，开发新产品，她应该遵循哪些步骤呢？
2. 开朗从哪些地方可以获得服装设计的灵感？

Supplementary Material

Product Life Cycle

The product life cycle (PLC) goes through many phases, involves many professional disciplines, and requires many skills, tools and processes. Product life cycle has to do with the life of a product in the market with respect to business/commercial costs and sales measures; whereas product lifecycle management (PLM) has more to do with managing descriptions and properties of a product through its development and useful life, mainly from a business/engineering point of view. To say that a product has a life cycle is to assert four things: ① products have a limited life; ② product sales pass through distinct stages, each posing different challenges, opportunities, and problems to the seller; ③ profits rise and fall at different stages of product life cycle; and ④ products require different marketing, financial, manufacturing, purchasing, and human resource strategies in each life cycle stage.

The different stages in a product life cycle are shown in the following diagram.

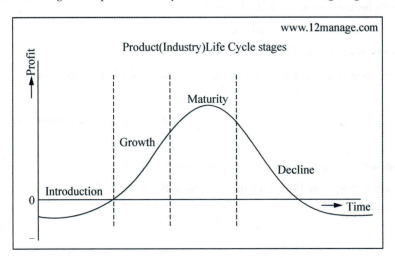

1. Market introduction stage
- Costs are high.
- Slow sales volumes to start.
- Little or no competition.
- Demand has to be created.
- Customers have to be prompted to try the product.

2. Growth stage
- Costs reduced due to economies of scale.
- Sales volume increases significantly.

- Profitability begins to rise.
- Public awareness increases.
- Competition begins to increase with a few new players in establishing market.
- Increased competition leads to price decreases.

3. Mature stage

- Costs are lowered as a result of production volumes increasing and experience curve effects.
- Sales volume peaks and market saturation is reached.
- More competitors entering the market.
- Prices tend to drop due to the competing products.
- Brand differentiation and feature diversification is emphasized to maintain or increase market share.
- Industrial profits go down.

4. Saturation and decline stage

- Costs become counter-optimal.
- Sales volume declines or stabilizes.
- Prices, profitability diminish.
- Profit becomes more a challenge of production/distribution efficiency than increased sales.

(Adapted from: http://www.quickmba.com/)

Questions

1. What are the stages of the Product Life Cycle?
2. On which stages are the following products in the PLC?

- digital camera
- thermos
- flash disc
- computer
- mobile phone

Unit 6

Branding

After learning this unit, you will be able to answer the following questions.

- How can we create brand loyalty?
- What is a brand?
- Branding
- How can a good brand name be decided?
- What are the branding strategies?

 Warm-up

"Branding program should be designed to differentiate your cow from all the other cattle on the range, even if all the cattle on the range look pretty much alike."

Can you list some famous brands in the cosmetic industry? How are they different from each other?

Reading 1

What Is A Brand?

The success of any business or consumer product depends in part on the target market's ability to distinguish one product from another. Branding is the main tool marketers use to distinguish their products from the competitors'.

A **brand** is a name, term, symbol, design, or combination thereof that identifies a seller's products and differentiates them from competitors' products. A **brand name** is that part of a brand that can be spoken, including letters (GM, LG, TCL), words (Chevrolet, Avon), and numbers (361°, 7–Eleven). The elements of a brand that cannot be spoken are called the **brand mark**. For example:

361° ANTA

BMW Benz

Benefits of Branding

Well-recognized brands make shopping easier. Think of trying to buy groceries, for example, if you had to evaluate the advantages and disadvantages of each of 25,000 items every time you went to a supermarket, it will be a torture. Many customers are willing to buy new things, but having gambled and won, they like to buy a sure thing the next time.

Brand promotion has advantages for branders as well as customers. A good brand reduces the marketer's selling time and effort. And sometimes a firm's brand name is the only element in its marketing mix that a competitor can't copy. Also, good brands can improve the company's image—speeding acceptance of new products marketed under the same name. For example, many consumers quickly tried Starbucks' coffee-flavored Frappuccino beverage when it appeared on grocery store shelves because they already knew they liked Starbuck's coffee.

Generally speaking, branding has three main purposes: product identification, repeat sales, and new-product sales. The most important purpose of branding is product identification. Branding allows marketers to distinguish their products from all others. Many brand names are familiar to consumers and indicate quality.

The second main purpose of branding is to generate repeat sales. The term **brand equity** refers to the value of company and brand names. A brand that has high awareness, perceived quality and brand loyalty among customers has high brand equity. A brand with strong brand equity is a valuable asset.

The best generator of repeat sales is satisfied customers. Branding helps consumers identify products they wish to buy again and avoid those they do not. **Brand loyalty**, a consistent preference for one brand over all others, is quite high in some product categories. Over half the users in product categories such as cigarettes, facial cream, toothpaste, coffee, headache remedies, photographic film, bath soap and cell phone are loyal to one brand. Brand identity is essential to developing brand loyalty.

The third main purpose of branding is to facilitate new-product sales. Famous brands are extremely useful when introducing new products.

The Internet provides firms a new alternative for generating brand awareness, promoting a desired brand image, stimulating new and repeat brand sales, and enhancing brand loyalty and building brand equity. A number of packaged goods firms, such as Procter & Gamble, and Gerber, have a presence on-line. Unilever's Lipton Recipe Secrets has launched a web site that will be a part of an interactive test in which the company plans to measure brand awareness, attitudes, and product usage as a result of consumers' exposure to the site.

(Adapted from Charles W. Lamb, et al., *Marketing*, 6th Edition, South-Western Educational Publishing, 2002, Chapter 9.)

Notes

① Brand: a name, term, symbol, design, or combination thereof that identifies a seller's products and differentiates them from competitors' products 品牌

② Brand name: part of a brand that can be spoken, including letters (GM), words (Chevrolet) and numbers (361°) 品牌名称

③ Brand mark: the elements of a brand that cannot be spoken 品牌标志

④ Brand equity: the value of company and brand names 品牌资产 / 品牌权益

⑤ Brand loyalty: a consistent preference for one brand over all others 品牌忠诚度

Discussion

1. Is a well-known brand valuable only to the owner of the brand?
2. Is there any difference between a brand name and a brand mark? If so, why is this

difference important?

3. Discuss with your classmates about your favorite brands and tell him/her why you are loyal to these brands?

4. List five brand names and indicate what product is associated with the brand name. Evaluate the strengths and weaknesses of the brand name.

 Reading 2

Branding Strategies

Firms face complex branding decisions. As Exhibit 6.1 illustrates, the first decision is whether to brand at all. Some firms actually use the lack of a brand name as a selling point. These unbranded products are called **generic products**. Firms that decide to brand their products may choose to follow a policy of using manufacturer's brands, private (distributor) brands, or both. In either case, they must then decide among a policy of individual branding (different brands for different products), family branding (common names for different products), or a combination of individual branding and family branding.

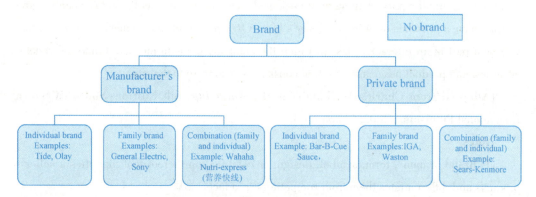

Exhibit 6.1 Major Branding Decisions

Generic products versus branded products

A **generic product** is typically a no-frills, no-brand-name, low-cost product that is simply identified by its product category. (Note that a generic product and a brand name that becomes generic, such as cellophane, are not the same thing.) Generic products have captured significant market shares in some product categories, such as canned fruits, canned vegetables, and paper products. These unbranded products are frequently identified only by black stenciled lettering on white packages.

The main appeal of generics is their low price. Generic grocery products are usually 30 to 40 percent less expensive than manufacturer's brands in the same product category and 20 to 25 percent less expensive than retailer-owned brands. For example:

Several Competing Generic Colas from the 1980s

Manufacturer's Brands versus Private Brands

The brand name of a manufacturer—such as Kodak, Panasonic, Haier—is called a **manufacturer's brand**. Sometimes the term "national brand" is used as a synonym for "manufacturer's brand". This term is not always accurate, however, because many manufactures serve only regional markets. The term manufacturer's brand more precisely defines the brand's owner.

A **private brand** is a brand name owned by a wholesaler or a retailer. Wal-Mart (沃尔玛), Carrefour (家乐福), and Lotus (易初莲花) are all private brands. Private brands now account for over 20 percent of sales at all U.S. mass merchandisers, drugstores, and supermarkets. Nowadays, the growth of store brands is greater than that of national brands. Marketing experts predict private labels to make up as much as 30 percent of grocery sales within five years—particularly as the consolidation continues among big supermarkets.

Individual Brands versus Family Brands

Many companies use different brand names for different products, a practice referred to as **individual branding**. Companies use individual brands when their products vary greatly in use or performance. For instance, Procter & Gamble (P&G) targets different segments of the laundry detergent market with Bold, Cheer, Dash, Dreft, Era, Gain, Ivory Snow, Oxydol, Solo, Ariel and Tide.

On the other hand, a company that markets several different products under the same brand name is using a **family brand**. Sony's family brand includes radios, television sets, stereos and other electronic products.

Co-branding

Co-branding entails placing two or more brand names on a product or its package. There are two types of co-branding. Ingredient branding identifies the brand of a part that makes up the product. Examples of ingredient branding are Intel (a microprocessor) in a personal computer, such as Compaq, or a premium leather interior (Coach) in an automobile (Lincoln). Cooperative branding is where two brands receive equal treatment on each other's brand equity, such as Citroen and Sony Ericsson.

Whatever branding strategy one picks, be aware that it may affect the branding and marketing of your company and other products. If you only have one product right now, your choice will mostly be whether you are going to brand the product with your company or not. Once you have a branding strategy in mind, it makes marketing and advertising decisions much easier.

(Adapted from Charles W. Lamb, et al., *Marketing*, 6th Edition, South-Western Educational Publishing, 2002, Chapter 9.)

Notes

① Generic product: a no-frills, no-brand-name, low-cost product that is simply identified by its product category 非商标(非专利)产品

② Manufacturers' brand: the brand name of a manufacturer 制造商品牌

③ Private brand: a brand name owned by a wholesaler or a retailer 自有品牌

④ Individual branding: using different brand names for different products 个别品牌

宝洁公司开发了11种不同品牌的洗衣粉，每种洗衣粉在市场上都有其独特的地位：汰渍(Tide)：洗涤能力强，去污彻底；奇尔(Cheer)：强劲的洗涤能力和护色能力；波德(Bold)：洗涤剂加织物柔软剂；格尼(Gain)：阳光一样的除味配方；时代(Era)：污渍处理，能有效去除污渍；达诗(Dash)：价值品牌；奥克多(Oxydol)：含有漂白剂配方，能有效漂白；梭罗(Solo)：洗涤剂与织物柔软剂的液体配方；卓夫特(Dreft)：婴儿衣物的杰出洗涤剂，并能保护柔嫩肌肤；象牙雪(Ivory Snow)：适合洗涤婴儿衣物和精细衣物，保护纤维和皮肤；碧浪(Ariel)：洗涤能力强，以西班牙语人群为目标市场。

⑤ Family brand: marketing several different products under the same brand name 统一品牌

⑥ Co-branding: placing two or more brand names on a product or its package 联合品牌

Group Discussion

1. Go to the Procter & Gamble website (www.pg.com) and click on Product List and Info and then on Beauty Care. Find out the brand names of the different shampoos that P & G makes. How are the different brands positioned, and what target markets do they appeal to?

2. A new soft drink company wants to be on the cutting edge of the sports drink industry. They have an idea for a sports energy drink that would cater to athletes of different sports. Help create a brand name and mark for this new sports energy drink.

 Activity 1

How to Pick up a Good Brand Name?

What constitutes a good brand name? Most effective brand names have several of the following features.

- Is easy to pronounce (by both domestic and foreign buyers);
- Is easy to recognize;
- Is easy to remember;
- Is short;
- Is distinctive, unique;
- Describes the product;
- Describes product use;
- Describes product benefits;
- Has a positive connotation;
- Reinforces the desired product image;
- Is legally protectable in home and foreign markets of interest.

Obviously no brand exhibits all of these characteristics. The most important issue is that the brand can be protected for exclusive use by its owner.

Discussion

1. Identify at least three outstanding brand names in each category, and explain why each is included in your list.

Product Category	Brands
Adhesive bandages	Band–Aid, Yunnan Baiyao, Johnson & Johnson, Watson's
Automobile	
Shampoo	

Beverage	
Cookie	
Computer	
Tobacco	
Facial cream	
Cell phone	
Alcohol	
Sports shoes	
Clothing	

What do you think about a good brand name?

2. A breakthrough in technology will now allow customers to use their cell phones while at the same time listening to music. Through the integration of the ipod technology and cell phone, customers can now hold a conversation while at the same time listening to music they have downloaded onto the ipod feature of the phone. The person on the other line will not be able to hear the music. Develop a brand name and brand mark for this new type of cellphone.

 Activity 2

I'll tell you why I like the cigarette business. It cost a penny to make. Sell it for a dollar. It's addictive. And there's a fantastic brand loyalty.

—Warren Buffet

How to Create Brand Loyalty?

What is Brand Loyalty?

Brand loyalty is a consumer's preference to buy a particular brand in a product category. It occurs because consumers perceive that the brand offers the right product features, images, or level of quality at the right price. This perception becomes the foundation for a new buying habit. Basically, consumers initially will make a trial purchase of the brand and, after satisfaction, tend to form habits and continue purchasing the same brand because the product is safe and familiar.

Brand loyalists have the following mindset.
- I am committed to this brand.

● I am willing to pay a higher price for this brand over other brands.

● I will recommend this brand to others.

What is the Process to Create and Maintain Brand Loyalty?

Favorable brand attitudes are the determinants of brand loyalty—consumers must like the product in order to develop loyalty to it. In order to convert occasional purchasers into brand loyalists, habits must be reinforced. Consumers must be reminded of the value of their purchase and encouraged to continue purchasing the product in the future.

To encourage repeat purchases, advertisement before and after the sale is critical. In addition to creating awareness and promoting initial purchases, advertising shapes and reinforces consumer attitudes so these attitudes mature into beliefs, which need to be reinforced until they develop into loyalty. For example, the most avid readers of a travel ad are those who just returned from the destination. Ads reinforce a traveler's perception and behavior. Remember, it is easier to reinforce behaviors than to change them and the sale is just the beginning of an opportunity to turn the purchaser into a loyalist.

A few more points to keep in mind…

● Develop an unbeatable product—if you want to keep customers, make sure they can get what they want from your product.

● Give customers an incentive to repeat-purchase—chance to win a prize, gift with a certain number of proofs of purchase, in-pack discount coupon, etc.

● Stand behind your product—if customers don't trust the product, they won't purchase it again.

● Know your trophy customers and treat them best of all—remember the rule that 80% of sales will come from the top 20% of customers.

● Make it easier to buy your brand than competing brands—availability and simplicity are keys in today's high-speed world. Customers appreciate convenience more than ever.

● Go to your customers—bring the product to customers when possible.

● Become a customer service champion—seek to serve the customer and they will repeat-purchase…again and again!

(By Nancy Giddens & Amanda Hofmann)

Just Do a Marketing Action!

Work in a group and go out to find the users of the following brands, ask them why they choose the brand. You might not be able to find users of all the listed brands. Just try your best to find as many as possible the different brand users.

Brands	How long have you used the brand	Why do you choose the brand	Brands	How long have you used the brand	Why do you choose the brand
Geely 吉利			Lexus 丰田 雷克萨斯		
Audi 奥迪			BYD 比亚迪		
BMW 宝马			Mazda 马自达		
Volvo 沃尔沃			Mercedes-Benz 奔驰		
Chevrolet 雪佛兰			Mitsubishi 三菱		
Honda 本田			Nissan 尼桑		

Ford 福特			Chery 奇瑞		
昌河铃木			Citroen 雪铁龙		
Jeep 北京吉普			Volkswagen 大众		
Buick 别克			Peugeot 标致		

Activity 3

Translation and Discussion (6)

Translate the following story and the questions into English, and then discuss the questions in English.

三人一致同意开朗的想法，决定创立自己的品牌。经过观察，他们发现中年职业女性没有很多时间逛商店，买衣服时喜欢认准一个店或一个品牌来购买。他们决定店名要与自己的服装品牌同名，同时店面的装修也要体现服装的整体风格。

问题

1. 你认为他们的服装品牌取一个什么名称好呢？
2. 你认为他们创立自己品牌的意义在哪里？有什么风险吗？

Supplementary Material

Haier: Taking a Brand Name Higher

It's "High-er," explains Michael Jemal, for what one assumes is the umpteenth time. "As in higher and higher." To Jemal, president of giant Chinese appliance maker Haier Group's American operations, the pronunciation is vital. In China as well as the U.S., Haier tends to come out more like "hair". And studies show most Americans associate Chinese brands with shoddy quality.

That's a perception Jemal is fighting mightily in his bid to make Haier the next premier name in white goods. Haier follows a playbook borrowed from the Japanese and Koreans: First, build a huge base at home that gives you economy of scale and a market where you can test products and perfect your manufacturing. Then go on the offensive overseas and race up the value chain. Thanks largely to its leadership in China, Haier is the world's fourth-largest home appliance maker, with 2005 sales of $12.8 billion. Since entering the U.S. in 1999, it has become the top-selling brand of compact refrigerators, a market leader in home wine coolers, and No. 3 in freezers. U.S. sales last year: $750 million. But Haier is still known in the U.S. mainly for commodity goods. "When I look across the major appliance categories, I've not yet seen [Haier] have any perceivable position," sniffs David L. Swift, Whirlpool Corp.'s boss for North America.

To change that, Haier is unveiling a line of eco-friendly, tech-rich appliances priced at $600 to $1,500, compared with the $200-to-$300 range it's known for. There's the Genesis top-loading washing machine, starting at around $725, and a dishwasher with food particle sensors to determine when plates are clean. "They won't be able to transform their image quickly, but it can be done," says Bob Walsh, chief operating officer of Fairfield (N.J.) Karl's Sales & Service, which stocks the Genesis washer.

Sharp competition in China has sliced into Haier's margins. But there's still reason to think the company has a shot. It has 50,000 workers in 46 factories, including a plant in Camden, S.C., and a massive complex in the coastal city of Qingdao, turning out more than 43 million products, from full-size fridges to digital TVs. This base gives Haier the heft to get new products to market quickly to fill any niche. "We used all our resources to get into the market at the low end, and then we crept into the midrange," says Jemal. "Now we are entering a new strategic phase."

(By Pete Engardio & Michael Arndt)

Questions

1. How much do you know about Haier? Find out the brand stories of Haier from the Internet and then share them with your classmates.

2. What has the Haier Group done to create brand loyalty?

Unit 7

Packaging

After learning this unit, you will be able to answer the following questions.

- What is green packaging
- What are the functions of packaging?
- What should be considered in the packaging decision?
- What is the importance of labeling?
- What is labeling?

Warm-up

Look at the pictures below. Beverages are packed in different shapes and sizes with different packaging materials. Do you know why? How many reasons can you list?

Reading 1

What Are the Functions of Packaging?

Packages have always served a practical function—that is, they hold contents together and protect goods as they move through the distribution channel. Today, however, packaging is also a container for promoting the product and making it easier and safer to use.

The three most important functions of packaging are to contain and protect products, to promote products, and to facilitate the storage, use, and convenience of products.

Containing and Protecting Products

The most obvious function of packaging is to contain products that are liquid, granular, or otherwise divisible. Packaging also enables manufacturers, wholesalers and retailers to market products in specific quantities, such as ounces.

Physical protection is another obvious function of packaging. Most products are handled several times between the time they are manufactured, harvested or otherwise produced and the time they are consumed or used. Many products are shipped, stored and inspected several times between production and consumption. Some, like milk, need to be refrigerated. Others, like beer, are sensitive to light. Still others, like medicines and bandages, need to be kept sterile. Packages protect products from breakage, evaporation, spillage, spoilage, light, heat, cold, infestation, and many other conditions.

Promoting Products

Packaging does more than identify the brand, list the ingredients, specify features, and give directions. A package differentiates a product from competing products and may associate a new product with a family of other products from the same manufacturer. **Welch's** repackaged its line of grape juice-based jams, jellies and juices to unify the line and get more impact on the shelf.

Packages use designs, colors, shapes and materials to try to influence consumers' perceptions and buying behavior. For example, marketing research shows that health-conscious consumers are likely to think that any food is probably good for them as long as it comes in green packaging.

Packaging has a measurable effect on sales. **Quaker Oats** revised the package for Rice-a-Roni without making any other changes in marketing strategy and experienced a 44 percent increase in sales in one year.

Facilitating Storage, Use, and Convenience

Wholesalers and retailers prefer packages that are easy to ship, store, and stock on shelves. They also like packages that protect products, prevent spoilage or breakage, and extend the product's shelf life.

Consumers' requirements for convenience cover many dimensions. Consumers are constantly seeking items that are easy to handle, open, and reclose, although some consumers want packages that are tamperproof or childproof. Consumers also want reusable and disposable packages. Surveys conducted by Sales & Marketing Management magazine revealed that consumers dislike—and avoid buying—leaky ice cream boxes, overly heavy or fat vinegar bottles, immovable pry-up lids on glass bottles, key-opener sardine cans, and hard-to-pour cereal boxes. Such packaging innovations as zipper tear strips, hinged lids, tab slots, screw-on tops, and pour spouts were introduced to solve these and other problems.

(Adapted from Charles W. Lamb, et al., *Marketing*, 6th Edition, South-Western Educational Publishing, 2002, Chapter 9.)

Notes

① Welch's(美国伟惜): Welch Foods Inc. is an American company, headquartered in Concord, Massachusetts. It is owned by the National Grape Cooperative Association, a cooperation of grape growers. Welch's is particularly known for its grape juices and jellies made from dark Concord grapes and its white Niagara grape juice.

② Quaker Oats(桂格麦片): The Quaker Oats Company is an American food conglomerate based in Chicago. In August 2001, Quaker merged with PepsiCo., Inc.

Discussion

1. What are the functions of packaging?

2. Find a product at home that has a distinctive package. Have a discussion evaluating that package based on the three functions of packaging discussed in the text.

3. Give an example where packaging costs probably lower total distribution costs or raise total distribution costs.

Reading 2

What Is Labeling?

An integral part of any package is its label. Labeling generally takes one of two forms: persuasive or informational. Persuasive labeling focuses on a promotional theme or logo, and consumer information is secondary. **Price Pfister** developed a new, persuasive label—featuring a picture of a faucet, the brand name, and the logo—with the goal of strengthening brand identity and becoming known as a brand instead of as a manufacturer. Note that the standard promotional claims—such as "new" "improved" and "super"—are no longer very persuasive. Consumers have been saturated with "newness" and thus discount these claims.

Informational labeling, in contrast, is designed to help consumers make proper product selections and lower their cognitive dissonance after the purchase. Sears attaches a "label of confidence" to all its floor coverings. This label gives such product information as durability, color, features, cleanability, care instructions, and construction standards. Most major furniture manufacturers affix labels to their wares that explain the products' construction features, such as type of frame, number of coils, and fabric characteristics. The U.S. Nutritional Labeling and Education Act of 1990 mandated detailed nutritional information on most food packages and standards for health claims on food packaging.

The Importance of Labeling

Most packages, whether final customer packaging or distribution packaging, are imprinted with information intended to assist the customer. For consumer products, labeling decisions are extremely important for the following reasons.

● Labels serve to capture the attention of shoppers. The use of catchy words may cause strolling customers to stop and evaluate the product.

● The label is likely to be the first thing a new customer sees and thus offers their first impression of the product.

● The label provides customers with product information to aid their purchase decision or help improve the customer's experience when using the product (e.g., recipes).

● Labels generally include a **universal product code** (UPC) and, in some cases, radio frequency identification (RFID) tags, that make it easy for resellers, such as retailers, to checkout customers and manage inventory.

● For companies serving international markets or diverse cultures within a single country, bilingual or multilingual labels may be needed.

● In some countries many products, including food and pharmaceuticals, are required by law to contain certain labels such as listing ingredients, providing nutritional information or including usage warning information.

Universal Product Codes

To speed handling of fast-selling products, governments and industry representatives have developed a universal product code that identifies each product with marks readable by electronic scanners. It was first introduced in 1974 on most items in supermarkets and other high-volume outlets. Because the numerical codes appear as a series of thick and thin vertical lines, they are often called **bar codes.**

The lines are read by computerized optical scanners that match codes with brand names, package sizes and prices. They also print information on cash registers tapes and help retailers rapidly and accurately prepare records of customer purchases, control inventories and track sales. Thus supermarkets and other high-volume retailers have been eager to use these codes. They speed the checkout process and reduce the need to mark the price on every item. They also reduce errors by cashiers and make it easy to control inventory and track sales of specific products.

(Adapted from Charles W. Lamb, et al., *Marketing*, 6th Edition, South-Western Educational Publishing, 2002; Paul Christ, *Know This: Marketing Basics*, 2nd Edition, KnowThis Media, 2012.)

Notes

① Price Pfister (飘菲): It is an American manufacturer of low to mid-range faucets and other plumbing products, and has been in business since 1915.

② Sears (西尔斯百货): Sears, sometimes known by its full name, Sears, Roebuck and Company, is an American mid-range chain of international department stores, founded by Richard Warren Sears and Alvah Roebuck in the late 19th century. From its mail order beginnings, the company grew to become the largest retailer in the United States by the mid-20th century.

③ universal product codes: 通用产品码(亦称条形码)。

Application

The FDA's website has a page on the food label requirements that proclaims "grocery store aisles have become avenues to greater nutritional knowledge." Go to that page at Internet address (*www.fda.gov/opacom/backgrounders/foodlabel/newlabel.html*) and review the actual label requirements. Do you use this information in deciding what products to buy?

Activity 1

What Should Be Considered in the Packaging Decision?

Along with protecting your product from light, oxygen, moisture, and handling, you will want to consider the following when choosing the right package.

- Protection—Packaging is used to protect the product from damage during shipping and handling, and to lessen spoilage if the protect is exposed to air or other elements.

- Visibility—Packaging design is used to capture customers' attention as they are shopping or glancing through a catalogue or website. This is particularly important for customers who are not familiar with the product and in situations, such as those found in grocery stores, where a product must stand out among thousands of other products. Packaging designs that stand out are more likely to be remembered on future shopping trips.

- Added Value—Packaging design and structure can add value to a product. For instance, benefits can be obtained from package structures that make the product easier to use while stylistic designs can make the product more attractive to display in customers' home.

- Distributor Acceptance—Packaging decisions must not only be accepted by the final customer, they may also have to be accepted by distributors who sell the product for the supplier. For instance, a retailer may not accept packages unless they conform to requirements they have for storing products on their shelves.

- Cost—Packaging can represent a significant portion of a product's selling price. For example, it is estimated that in the cosmetics industry the packaging cost of some products may be as high as 40% of a product's selling price. Smart packaging decisions can help reduce costs and possibly lead to higher profits.

- Expensive to Create—Developing new packaging can be extremely expensive. The costs involved in creating new packaging include graphic and structural design, production, customer testing, possible destruction of leftover old packaging, and possible advertising to inform customer of the new packaging.

- Long Term Decision—When companies create a new package, it is most often with the intention of having the design on the market for an extended period of time. In fact, changing a product's packaging too frequently can have negative effects since customers become conditioned to locate the product based on its package and may be confused if the design is altered.

● Technical requirements—How will the package be filled? Some chutney producers are demanding wide-mouthed squat jars.

● Environmental or Legal Issues—Packaging decisions must also include an assessment of its environmental impact especially for products with packages that are frequently discarded. Packages that are not easily bio-degradable could draw customer and possibly governmental concern. Also, caution must be exercised in order to create packages that do not infringe on intellectual property, such as copyrights, trademarks or patents, held by others.

(Adapted from Paul Christ, *Know This: Marketing Basics*, 2nd Edition, KnowThis Media, 2012.)

Application

1. Give examples where packaging costs probably lower total distribution costs or raise total distribution costs.

2. With reference to the factors mentioned above, comment on the following perfume packaging designs.

Brands	Products	Pictures
Dior 迪奥	迪奥小姐花漾淡香氛	
Chanel 香奈儿	5号香水	
Lancome 兰蔻	奇迹珍爱香水	

Estee Lauder 雅诗兰黛	欢沁女士香水	
Anna sui 安娜苏	幻境奇缘淡香水	
Marc Jacobs 马克·雅可布	雏菊女士香水	

 Activity 2

What Is Green Packaging?

Sweet things may come in pretty packages, but just how environmentally friendly is all that wrapping?

More and more packaging suppliers are producing recycled products that protect the environment and their costs. Such products are described as being either manufactured from recycled material or are themselves biodegradable. This packaging is called green (sustainable) packaging which is an immensely popular and positive trend nowadays.

Then what are the criteria of green (sustainable) packaging? The following criteria are usually considered.

- Is beneficial, safe & healthy for individuals and communities throughout its life cycle;
- Meets market criteria for performance and cost;
- Is sourced, manufactured, transported and recycled using renewable energy;
- Maximizes the use of renewable or recycled source materials;
- Is manufactured using clean production technologies and best practices;
- Is made from materials healthy in all probable end of life scenarios;
- Is physically designed to optimize materials and energy;
- Is effectively recovered and utilized in biological and/or industrial cradle to cycles.

All of us should make a responsible and positive choice in terms of packaging. We believe that by successfully addressing these criteria, packaging can be transformed into a cradle to cradle flow of packaging materials in a system that is economically robust and provides benefit throughout the life cycle—a sustainable packaging system.

Application

Guided by the above criteria, make your judgment on the following packaging. Are they green? If not, how could they be improved?

Example 1 The filling is straw.

Example 2 Different packaging designs of tea.

Example 3 The Chinese moon cake boxes are made of wood paper, tin or bamboo.

Activity 3

Translation and Discussion (7)

Translate the following story and the questions into English, and then discuss the questions in English.

要让顾客认可自己的品牌，除了服装设计要符合顾客的心理需求外，店面的装修及服装的包装也很重要。

问题

1. 你觉得服装的包装重要吗？包装的作用体现在哪些方面呢？
2. 请根据服装店所服务的顾客群特点，给出几点关于包装设计的建议，如包装袋的尺寸、颜色、质料等。

Supplementary Material

I. Packaging Types

Packaging may be looked at as several different types. For example, a **transport package or distribution package** can be the shipping container used to ship, store, and handle the product or inner packages. Some identify a **consumer package** as one which is directed toward a consumer or household.

Packaging may be discussed in relation to the type of product being packaged: medical device packaging, bulk chemical packaging, over-the-counter drug packaging, retail food packaging, military materiel packaging, pharmaceutical packaging, etc.

tin can with a pull tab

various household packaging types for foods

It is sometimes convenient to categorize packages by layer or function: "primary" "secondary", etc.

- Primary packaging is the material that first envelops the product and holds it. This usually is the smallest unit of distribution or use and is the package which is in direct contact with the contents.

● Secondary packaging is outside the primary packaging—perhaps used to group primary packages together.

● Tertiary packaging is used for bulk handling, warehouse storage and transport shipping. The most common form is a palletized unit load that packs tightly into containers.

These broad categories can be somewhat arbitrary. For example, depending on the use, a shrink wrap can be primary packaging when applied directly to the product, secondary packaging when combining smaller packages, and tertiary packaging on some distribution packs.

(Adapted from http://en.wikipedia.org/wiki)

II. Symbols Used on Packages and Labels

Many types of symbols for package labeling are nationally and internationally standardized. For consumer packaging, symbols exist for product certifications, trademarks, proof of purchase, etc. Some requirements and symbols exist to communicate aspects of consumer use and safety. Examples of environmental and recycling symbols include: ① Recycling symbol, ② Resin identification code, ③ and Green Dot (symbol). (as shown in the figures below)

Bar codes, Universal Product Codes and RFID labels are common to allow automated information management.

Shipping container labeling

Shipments of hazardous materials or dangerous goods have special information and symbols (labels, placards, etc.) as required by UN countries, and specific carrier requirements. Below are two examples of shipping container labels.

With transport packages, standardized symbols are also used to aid in handling. Some common ones are shown as below.

Clothing Wash Care Labels

While washing, you should pay attention to the meaning of care symbols in your clothes and other textiles. Here are some instructions.

WASHING INSTRUCTIONS

Machine Wash, COLD	Machine Wash, COLD Permanent Press(免烫)	Machine Wash, COLD Gentle Cycle
Hand Wash	Machine Wash, WARM	Machine Wash, WARM Permanent Press
Machine Wash, WARM Gentle Cycle	Do Not Wash	Machine Wash, HOT
Machine Wash, HOT Permanent Press	Machine Wash, HOT Gentle Cycle	

BLEACHING INSTRUCTIONS

Do Not Bleach	Bleach as needed	Non–chlorine Bleach as needed
No bleach product should be used including detergents with bleach or follow bleach package test procedures to test for bleach safety.	Any bleach, like Clorox®, may be safely used.	Use only a colour–safe bleach, like Clorox 2®.

DRYING INSTRUCTIONS

Tumble Dry, NO HEAT	Tumble Dry, Permanent Press NO HEAT	Tumble Dry, Gentle Cycle NO HEAT
Do Not Tumble Dry	Tumble Dry, LOW HEAT	Tumble Dry, Permanent Press LOW HEAT
Tumble Dry, Gentle Cycle LOW HEAT	Line Dry	Tumble Dry, MEDIUM

Tumble Dry, Permanent Press MEDIUM	Tumble Dry, Gentle Cycle MEDIUM	Drip Dry
Tumble Dry, HIGH	Dry Flat	

IRONING INSTRUCTIONS

Iron, Steam or Dry, with LOW HEAT	Do Not Iron with Steam
Iron, Steam or Dry, with MEDIUM HEAT	Do Not Iron
Iron, Steam or Dry, with HIGH HEAT	

DRYCLEANING INSTRUCTIONS

Dryclean — Take this item to a professional drycleaner.	Do Not Dryclean

Questions

1. Check the labels on your clothes and try to figure out their meanings.

2. Have you ever paid attention to the Resin Identification Code (塑胶分类标志) on the bottom of plastic bottles? On the bottom of mineral water bottles, there is usually a symbol ![PETE 1]; on the bottom of shampoo bottles, there is usually a symbol ![HDPE 2] … Do you know what they stand for? Surf on the Internet and find out the meanings of the following codes.

3. It is reported that a 12-year-old girl in Dubai died after long usage (16 months) of SAFA mineral water bottle. She used to carry the same fancy (painted by herself) bottle to her school daily. In a nutshell, the plastic (called polyethylene terephthalate or PET) used in these bottles contains a potentially carcinogenic element (something called diethyllydroxylamine or DEHA). The bottles are safe for one-time use only; if you must keep them longer, it should be no more than a few days, weeks max, and keep them away from heat as well. Repeated washing and rinsing can cause the plastic to break down and the carcinogens (cancer-causing chemical agents) can leak into the water that YOU are drinking. Better to invest in water bottles that are really meant for multiple uses.

What has the report taught you?

Unit 8

Pricing

After learning this unit, you will be able to answer the following questions.

- How can a price be adjusted
- What is price?
- How can the cost of a product be calvulated?
- Pricing
- How can a produce be priced?
- What should be considered when pricing a product?

Warm-up

1. What do the following words have in common? Fare, dues, tuition, interest, rent, and fee.

2. Are you price sensitive? Where in your city do you normally go to buy clothes and where do you not go? Why?

3. Usually clothes sold by department stores are more expensive than those

by small clothing stores. What do you think make the goods sold by department stores more expensive?

 Reading 1

What Is Price?

Price means one thing to the consumer and something else to the seller. To the consumer, it is the cost of something. To the seller, price is revenue, the primary source of profits. In the broadest sense, price allocates resources in a free-market economy. With so many ways of looking at price, it's no wonder that marketing managers find the task of setting prices a challenge.

Price is that which is given up in an exchange to acquire goods or service. Price is typically the money exchanged for the goods or service. It may also be time lost while waiting to acquire the goods or service. For example, many people waited all day at Southwest Airline's ticket counters during the company's twenty-fifth anniversary sale. Even then, some people didn't get the deeply discounted tickets that they had been hoping for. Price also might include "lost dignity" for an individual who loses his job and must rely on charity to obtain food and clothing.

Consumers are interested in obtaining a "reasonable price". "Reasonable price" really means "perceived reasonable value" at the time of the transaction and not necessarily the satisfaction they actually receive.

Price can relate to anything with perceived value, not just money. When goods and services are changed, the trade is called barter. For example, if you exchange this book for a chemistry book at the end of the term, you have engaged in barter. The price you paid for the chemistry book was this textbook.

The Importance of Price to Marketing Managers

Prices are the key to revenues, which in turn are the key to profits for an organization. Revenue is the price charged to customers multiplied by the number of units sold. Revenue is what pays for every activity of the company: production, finance, sales, distribution, and so on. What's left over (if anything) is profit. Managers usually strive to charge a price that will earn a fair profit.

To earn a profit, managers must choose a price that is not too high or too low, a price that equals the perceived value to target consumers. If a price is set too high in consumers' minds, the perceived value will be less than the cost, and sales opportunities will be lost. Many mainstream purchasers of cars, sporting goods, CDs, tools, wedding gowns, and computers are buying "used or preowned" items to get a better deal.

Lost sales mean lost revenue. Conversely, if a price is too low, it may be perceived as a great value for the consumer, but the firm loses revenue it could have earned. Setting prices too low may not even attract as many buyers as managers might think. One study surveyed over two thousand shoppers at national chains around the country and found that over 60 percent intended to buy full-price items only. Retailers that place too much emphasis on discount may not be able to meet the expectations of full-price customers.

(Adapted from Charles W. Lamb, et al., *Marketing*, 6th Edition, South-Western Educational Publishing, 2002, Chapter 17.)

Discussion

How important is price to the products?

 Reading 2

How to Price a Product?

When marketing managers establish pricing goals, they must set specific prices to reach those goals. Marketers have at their disposal several approaches for setting the initial price which include:

- Cost Pricing
  - Markup Pricing
  - Cost-Plus Pricing
  - Breakeven Pricing
- Market Pricing
  - Backward Pricing
  - Psychological Pricing
  - Price Lining
- Competitive Pricing
- Bid Pricing

COST PRICING

Under cost pricing the marketer primarily looks at production costs as the key factor in determining the initial price.

The idea of cost may seem simple, but it is actually a multifaceted concept, especially for producers of goods and services. A **variable cost** (VC) is a cost that deviates with changes in the level of output; and example of a variable cost is the cost of materials. In contrast, a **fixed cost** (FC) does not change as output is increased or decreased. Examples include rent and executives' salaries.

In order to compare the cost of production to the selling price of a product, it is helpful to calculate costs per unit, or average costs. **Average total cost (ATC)** equals total costs divided by quantity of output. In the simplest case, the total cost function is expressed as follows, where Q represents the production quantity, VC represents variable costs, FC represents fixed costs.

$$ATC = \frac{FC + VC}{Q}$$

Markup Pricing

Markup pricing, the most popular method used by wholesalers and retailers to establish a selling price, does not analyze the costs of production. Instead, markup pricing is the cost of buying the product from the producer, plus amounts for profit and for expenses not otherwise accounted for. The total determines the selling price.

A retailer, for example, adds a certain percentage to the cost of the merchandise received to arrive at the retail price. An item that costs the retailer $1.80 and is sold for $2.20 carries a markup of 40¢, which is a markup of 22 percent of the cost (40¢ ÷ $1.80). Retailers tend to discuss markup in terms of its percentage of the retail price—in this example, 18 percent (40¢ ÷ $2.20), the difference between the retailer's cost and the selling price 40¢ is the gross margin.

Markups are based on experience. For example, many small retailers mark up merchandise 100 percent over cost. (In other words, they double the cost.) This tactic is called **keystoning**. Some other factors that influence markups are the merchandise's appeal to customers, past response to the markup (an implicit demand consideration), the item's promotional value, the seasonality of the goods, their fashion appeal, the product's traditional selling price, and competition.

The biggest advantage of markup pricing is its simplicity. The pricing disadvantage is that it ignores demand and may result in overpricing or underpricing the merchandise.

Cost-Plus Pricing

In the same way markup pricing arrives at price by adding a certain percentage to the product's cost, cost-plus pricing also adds to the cost by using a fixed monetary amount rather than percentage. For instance, a contractor hired to renovate a homeowner's bathroom will estimate the cost of doing the job by adding their total labor cost to the cost of the materials used in the renovation. The homeowner's selection of ceramic tile to be used in the bathroom is likely to have little effect on the labor needed to install it whether it is a low-end, low priced tile or a high-end, premium priced tile. Assuming most material in the bathroom project are standard sizes and configuration, any change in the total price for the renovation is a result of changes in material costs while labor costs are constant.

If you are in the USA, it should be noted carefully that any pricing on a cost–plus contract can be audited by the government. How to do this pricing, what items can be included, and how the calculations are to be made is governed by the FAR (or Federal Acquisition Regulations). Failure to follow the precepts of FAR can lead to decreased contractor revenue or, in extreme cases, claims of penalties against the contractor under the *False Claims Act* and *Contract Disputes Act*.

Breakeven Pricing

Breakeven pricing is associated with breakeven analysis, which is a forecasting tool used by marketers to determine how many products must be sold before the company starts realizing a profit.

Let's see an example of calculating the break–even point for a firm with the following graphic. A firm's break–even point occurs when at a point where total revenue equals total costs.

Formula: Q= FC / (UP – VC)

(Q = Break–even Point, i.e., Units of production, FC = Fixed Costs, VC = Variable Costs per Unit , UP = Unit Price)

Therefore,

Break–Even Point Q = Fixed Cost / (Unit Price – Variable Unit Cost)

For example, assume a company operates a single–product manufacturing plant that has a total fixed cost (e.g. purchase of equipment, mortgage, etc.) per year of (US) $3,000,000 and the variable cost (e.g. raw materials, labor, electricity, etc.) is $45.00 per unit. If the company sells the product directly to customers for $120, it will require the company to sell 40,000 units to break even.

$$\frac{\$3,000,000}{\$120 - \$45} = 40,000 \text{ units}$$

Again we must emphasize that marketers must determine whether the demand (i.e. number of units needed to break even) is realistically attainable. Simply plugging in a number for price without knowing how the market will respond to that figure means that this method has little value. (Note: A common mistake when performing this analysis is to report the breakeven in a monetary value such a breakeven in dollars (e.g. $40,000). The calculation presented above is a measure of units that need to be sold. Clearly it is easy to turn this into a revenue breakeven analysis by multiplying the units needed by the selling price. In our example, 40,000 units × $120 = $4,800,000.

MARKET PRICING

Market pricing is one of the most common methods for setting price, and the one that seems most logical given marketing's focus on satisfying customers. The main goal is to learn what customers in an organization's target market are likely to perceive as an acceptable price. Of course this price should also help the organization meet its marketing objectives. Market pricing has several types: psychological pricing, backward pricing, and price lining.

Backward Pricing

In some marketing organizations the price the market is willing to pay for a product is an important determinant of many other marketing decisions. This is likely to occur when the market has a clear perception of what it believes is an acceptable level of pricing.

In situations where a price range is ingrained in the market, the marketer may need to use this price as the starting point for many decisions and work backwards to develop product, promotion and distribution plans. For instance, assume a company sells products through retailers. If the market is willing to pay (US)$199 for a product but is resistant to pricing that is higher, the marketer will work backwards factoring out the profit margin retailers are likely to want (e.g. $40) and as well as removing the marketer's profit (e.g. $70). From this, the product cost will remain ($199-$40-$70= $89). The marketer must then decide whether they can create a product with sufficient features and benefits to satisfy customers' needs at this cost level.

Psychological Pricing

Psychological pricing or price ending is a marketing practice based on the theory that certain prices have a psychological impact. The retail prices are often expressed as "odd prices" : a little less than a round number, e.g. $19.99 or £6.95 (but not necessarily mathematically odd, it could also be 2.98). The theory is this drives demand greater than what would be expected if consumers were perfectly rational.

Price Lining

Price lining is the use of a limited number of prices for all the product offerings. This is a tradition started in the old five and dime stores in which everything cost either 5 or 10 cents. Its underlying rationale is that these amounts are seen as suitable price points for a whole range of products by prospective customers. It has the advantage of ease of administering, but the disadvantage of inflexibility, particularly in times of inflation or unstable prices.

COMPETITIVE PRICING

As we noted, how competitors price their products can influence the marketer's pricing decision. Clearly when setting price it makes sense to look at the price of competitive offerings. In some industries, particularly those in which there are a few dominant competitors and many small companies, the top companies are in the position of holding price leadership roles where they are often the first in the industry to change price. Smaller companies must then assume a price follower role and react once the big companies adjust their price.

When basing pricing decisions on how competitors are setting their price, firms may follow one of the following approaches: Below Competition Pricing, Above Competition Pricing, Parity Pricing.

BID PRICING

Not all selling situations allow the marketer to have advanced knowledge of the prices offered by competitors. While the Internet has made researching competitor pricing a relatively routine exercise, this is not the case in markets where bid pricing occurs. Bid pricing typically requires a marketer to submit a price to a potential buyer that is sealed or unseen by competitors. It is not until all bids are obtained and unsealed that the marketer is informed of the price listed by competitors.

Bid pricing occurs in several industries though it is a standard requirement when selling to local, national and international governments. In these situations the marketer's pricing strategy depends on the projected winning bid price, which is generally the lowest price. However, price alone is only the deciding factor if the bidder meets certain qualifications. The fact that marketers often operate in the dark in terms of available competitor research, makes this type of pricing one of the most challenging of all pricing setting methods.

(Adapted from Paul Christ, *Know This: Marketing Basics*, 2nd Edition, KnowThis Media, 2012, Chapter 18.)

Discussion

1. What are the advantages and disadvantages of the pricing approaches mentioned in the text?

2. Men's shirts can be priced from tens to hundreds even thousands of RMB. What do you think makes the price differ so much?

3. If you are going to run a bakery near a school, how will you price your products?

4. Which pricing approach is probably most appropriate for each of the following products? (a) a nationally advertised chocolate bar; (b) a skin parch drug to help smokers quit; (c) a DVD of a best-selling movie; (d) a new children's toy.

Notes

① Variable cost, also known as operating costs, prime costs, on costs and direct costs, are costs which vary directly with the level of output, e.g. labour, fuel, power and cost of raw material. 可变成本

② Fixed costs are costs which do not vary with output, e.g. rent. 固定成本

③ Average total cost is the total cost divided by the quantity of output. 平均成本

④ Average fixed cost is the fixed cost divided by the quantity of output. 平均固定成本

⑤ Average variable cost is variable costs divided by the quantity of output. 平均可变成本

⑥ Cost-plus pricing: works well when the buyer and seller don't know what the cost of production will be but agree to a target profit over and above the product cost. 溢价定价法

⑦ Mark-up pricing: the percentage of profit is added to the per unit cost to set product price. 成本加成定价法

⑧ Marginal cost: the change in total costs associated with a one-unit change in output. 边际成本

⑨ Keystoning: the practice of marking up prices by 100 percent, or doubling the cost. 加倍定价法

 Activity 1

What to Consider When Pricing a Product?

Effective pricing of products is an art. Reaching that delicate balance between consumer demand and product value generally takes a great deal of research and insight. But those business owners who continually invest in this process will position their businesses to maximize the revenue potential from their customers and ultimately increase their bottom line.

When trying to price the products in your business, there are several things to consider, which are as follows.

What are you selling? Your first consideration when determining your pricing strategy is to take a look at the products themselves. Are you offering a high-end or specialized item, or something more generic? If the price of a high-end or specialized product is set too low compared to competitive products, then customers will perceive that the quality is lower. On the other hand, a standard product that is significantly higher in price compared to those of competitors may drive away customers who feel the product is overpriced.

Who is your target market? Who shops at your business, what products and services are they looking for, and what are their spending habits? Since pricing is directly linked to consumer demand, awareness of the current consumer trends is invaluable to running a successful small business.

What is your competitor doing? In order to properly price your products and services it is essential that you determine what your competitors are charging and what the customers get for their money in terms of value and service. This information should give you a general price range for the products and services you are offering.

What is your business's perceived value among customers? The value of your products is greater than raw materials and labor that was used to create them. Convenience, customer service, free or immediate shipping, location, brand name, and reputation all add to the value of your products and will affect how much a customer is willing to pay for them.

How should your salespeople close a deal? To encourage consistency and quality performance from your salespeople, you should create price guidelines that contain a target price, price floor and price ceiling, and then only allow deals that fall within this range. You should also create an incentive program that rewards high profit margins over sales volume, since salespeople may try to sell products and services at the lowest possible price in order to close the deal.

Application

Suppose you are going to provide a tutoring service. Guided by the questions above, do the necessary research and then decide the price of your service. Tell your classmates why you price your service like that.

Activity 2

How to Adjust a Price?

The final price may be further adjusted through promotional pricing. Unlike standard adjustments, which are often permanently part of a marketer's pricing strategy and may include either a decrease or increase in price, promotional pricing is a temporary adjustment that only involves price reductions. In most cases this means the marketer is selling the product at levels that significantly reduce the profit they make per unit sold.

The options for promotional pricing include the following.
- Markdowns
- Loss Leaders
- Sales Promotions
- Bundle Pricing
- Dynamic Pricing

Markdowns

The most common method for stimulating customer interest using price is the promotional markdown method, which offers the product at a price that is lower than the product's normal selling price. There are several types of markdowns, including the following.

Temporary Markdown—Possibly the most familiar pricing method marketers use to generate sales is to offer a temporary markdown or "sale" pricing. These markdowns are normally for a specified period of time, the conclusion of which will result in the product being raised back to the normal selling price.

Permanent Markdown—Unlike the temporary markdown where the price will eventually be raised back to a higher price, the permanent markdown is intended to move the product out of inventory. This type of markdown is used to remove old products which: are perishable and close to being out of date (e.g. donuts); are an older model and must be sold to make room for new models; or are products that the marketer no longer wishes to sell.

Seasonal—Products that are primarily sold during a particular time of the year, such as clothing, gardening products, sporting goods and holiday-specific items, may see price reductions at the conclusion of its prime selling season.

Loss Leaders

An important type of pricing program used primarily by retailers is the loss leader. Under this method a product is intentionally sold at or below the cost the retailer pays to acquire the product from suppliers. The idea is that offering such a low price will entice a high level of customer traffic to visit a retailer's store or website. The expectation is that customers will easily make up for the profit lost on the loss leader item by purchasing other items that are not following loss leader pricing. For instance, a convenience store may advertise a very low price for cups of coffee in order to generate traffic to the store with the hope that customers will purchase regularly priced products to go along with the coffee purchase.

Marketers should beware that some governmental agencies view loss leaders as a form of predatory pricing and thus consider it illegal. Predatory pricing occurs when an organization is deliberately selling products at or below cost with the intention of driving competitors out of business. Of course, this differs from our discussion which considers loss leader pricing as a form of promotion and not a form of anti-competitor activity. In the U.S., several state governments have passed laws under the heading *Unfair Sales Act*, which prohibits the selling of certain products below cost. The main intention of these laws is to protect small firms from below-cost pricing activities of larger companies. Some states place this restriction on specific product categories (e.g., gasoline, tobacco) but Oklahoma places this restriction on most products and goes as far as requiring the pricing of products be at least 6% above cost.

Sales Promotions

As we noted, marketers may offer several types of pricing promotions to simulate demand. While we have already discussed "sale" pricing as a technique to build customer interest, there are several other sales promotions that are designed to lower price. These include rebates, coupons, trade-in, and loyalty programs.

Bundle Pricing

Another pricing adjustment designed to increase sales is to offer discounted pricing when customers purchase several different products at the same time. Termed bundle pricing, the technique is often used to sell products that are complementary to a main product. For buyers, the overall cost of the purchase shows a savings compared to purchasing each product individually. For example, a camera retailer may offer a discounted price when customers purchase both a digital camera and a how-to photography DVD that is lower than if both items were purchased separately. In this example the retailer may promote this as: "Buy both the digital camera and the how-to photography DVD and save 25%."

Bundle pricing is also used by marketers as a technique that avoids making price adjustments on a main product for fear that doing so could affect the product's perceived quality level. Rather, the marketer may choose to offer adjustments on other related or complementary products. In our example the message changes to: "Buy the digital camera and you can get the how-to photography DVD for 50% less." With this approach the marketer is presenting a price adjustment without the perception of lowering the price of the main product.

Dynamic Pricing

The concept of dynamic pricing has received a great deal of attention in recent years due to its prevalent use by Internet retailers. But the basic idea of dynamic pricing has been around since the dawn commerce. Essentially dynamic pricing allows for the point-of-sale (i.e., at the time and place of purchase) price adjustments to take place for customers meeting certain criteria established by the seller. The most common and oldest form of dynamic pricing is haggling; the give-and-take that takes place between buyer and seller as they settle on a price. While the word haggling may conjure up visions of transactions taking place among vendors and customers in a street market, the concept is widely used in business markets as well where it carries the more reserved label of negotiated pricing.

Advances in computer hardware and software present a new dimension for the use of dynamic pricing. Unlike haggling, where the seller makes price adjustments based on a person-to-person discussion with a buyer, dynamic pricing uses sophisticated computer technology to adjust price. It achieves this by combining customer data (e.g., who they are, how they buy) with pre-programmed price offerings that are aimed at customers meeting certain criteria. For example, dynamic pricing is used in retail stores where customers' use of loyalty cards triggers the store's computer to access customer information. If customers' characteristics match requirements in the software program they may be offered a special deal such as 10% off if they also purchase another product. Dynamic pricing is also widely used in airline ticket purchasing where type of customer (e.g., business vs. leisure traveler) and date of purchase can affect pricing.

On the Internet, marketers may use dynamic pricing to entice first time visitors to make a purchase by offering a one-time discount. This is accomplished by comparing information stored in the marketer's computer database with identifier information gathered as the person is visiting a website. One way this is done is for a website to leave small data files called "cookies" on a visitor's computer when they first access the marketer's website. A cookie can reside on the visitor's computer for some time and allows the marketer to monitor the user's behavior on the site such as how often they visit, how long they spend on the site, what WebPages they access and much more. The marketer can then program special software, often called campaign management software, to send visitors a special offer such as a discount. For instance, the marketer may have a discount offered if the visitor has come to the site at least five times in the last six months but has never purchased.

As one would expect, the main objective of promotional pricing is to stimulate product demand. But as we noted back, marketers should be careful not to overuse promotional programs that temporarily reduce selling price. If promotional pricing is used too frequently, customers may become conditioned to anticipate the reduction. This results in buyers withholding purchases until the product is again offered at a lower price. Since promotional pricing often means the marketing organization is making very little profit off of each item sold, consistently selling at a low price could jeopardize the company's ability to meet their financial objectives.

Discussion

Besides the methods mentioned above, there are many other ways, such as a two-for-one offer(买一送一), for example, KFC introduced other goods with their food like watches, keychains, etc. to the customers.

What other methods can you think of to adjust the prices?

Application

1. Suppose there are two rice noodle restaurants in one block. What could one restaurant do to attract more customers?

2. Suppose there is a new brand cell phone to be launched in the market this May, what measures can be taken to compete more effectively with those well-known brands such as Apple, Samsung…?

3. While buying cosmetics, what attracts you most? If you are to promote this product, what will you do?

Activity 3

Translation and Discussion (8)

Translate the following story and the questions into English, and then discuss the questions in English.

韩柳他们开始做自己的品牌服装，在自己的店面出售。同一款式、同一型号的服装一般只做两件，最多不超过四件。由于成本较高，服装的定价自然不低。不过，由于服装设计能体现中年职业女性的心理需求，所以他们的生意很不错。

问题
1. 他们服装的定价要考虑哪些因素？
2. 应该如何计算一件衣服的成本？

Supplementary Material

How to Calculate Cost of Goods

Marketing campaigns are investments. Like any smart investment, they need to be measured, monitored and compared to other investments to ensure you're spending your money wisely.

Return on investment (ROI) is a measure of the profit earned from each investment. Like the return you earn on your portfolio or bank account, it's calculated as a percentage. In simple terms, the calculation is

$$ROI = \frac{(Profit - Investment)}{Investment}$$

and

$$Profit = Revenue - Cost\ of\ goods\ sold\ (COGS)$$

ROI calculations for marketing campaigns can be complex—you may have many variables on both the profit side and the investment (cost) side. But understanding the formula is essential if you need to produce the best possible results with your marketing investments.

COGS is the actual cost to physically produce your company's product or service. Companies calculate COGS differently, so check with your finance or accounting team to get the formula they use. But if you're on your own, here's a way to calculate COGS for a product and then for a service.

COGS calculation for a product

Choose a timeframe for your calculation—you'll record or estimate your expenses over this period (month, quarter, year, etc.).

Data	Value	#
How much did you spend on raw materials during this timeframe?		A
What did you spend on labor to produce the product?		B
List the costs associated with the shipping & inventory of raw materials.		C
Production facility expenses if the facility is solely for this product (or you can use a percentage).		D
Some companies include an allocation for general overhead, such as customer service, order processing, or other items in the COGS figure. Enter the total for the timeframe.		E

Data	Value	#
TOTAL: Add A through E		F
Number of units sold during this period		G
Divide F by G—this is your COGS per unit.		H

COGS for a service

If you need COGS for a service, choose a timeframe for your calculation—you'll report or record your expenses over this period (month, quarter, year, etc.).

Data	Value	#
How much did you spend on labor to deliver the service over your chosen timeframe?		A
What did you spend on materials to deliver your service?		B
Are there any other variable costs associated with the delivery of your service?		C
Some companies include an allocation for general overhead, such as customer service, order processing, or other items in the COGS figure. Enter the total for the timeframe.		D
TOTAL: Add A through D		E
Number of services delivered (or customers serviced) during this period		F
Divide E by F—this is your COGS per unit.		G

Again, it's important to check with your accountant/finance expert to make sure you've calculated correctly for your company or industry — particularly if you're going to use the data for investment decisions.

(Adapted from: http://www.marketingmo.com/how-to-articles/)

Application

Visit a Bakery owner, and try to find out how to calculate the cost of a piece of bread.

Unit 9

Distribution

After learning this unit, you will be able to answer the following questions.

- When do conflicts happen among channel members?
- How can products be delivered to customers?
- Where can products be sold?
- Why are intermediaries needed?
- Who are intermediaries?

(Distribution)

 Warm-up

Eliminate the middleman and prices will come down!

What do you think of the statement? Assume that all of the marketing intermediaries are legally banned, what would a consumer have to do to get a bottle of shampoo?

 Reading 1

Distribution Channels

There are many channels a product can take to reach its final consumer. Marketers search for the most efficient channel from the many alternatives available. Exhibit 9.1 illustrates the ways manufacturers can route products to consumers. Usually, the product can reach the consumer directly or indirectly. Direct channels include telemarketing, mail-order, catalog shopping, and forms of electronic retailing like on-line shopping and shop-at-home television networks. Agent/broker channels are used in markets with many small manufacturers and many retailers that lack the resources to find each other. Most consumer products are sold through distribution channels similar to the other two alternatives: the retailer channel and the wholesaler channel.

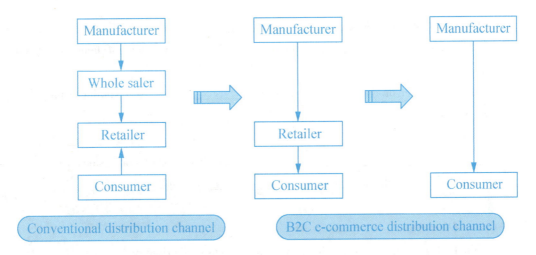

Exhibit 9.1 Marketing Channels

Formally, a marketing channel is a business structure of interdependent organization that reaches from the point of product origin to the consumer with the purpose of moving products to their final consumption destination. Marketing channels facilitate the physical movement of goods through the supply chain, representing "place" in the marketing mix and encompassing the processes involved in getting the right product to the right place at the right time.

Many different types of organizations participate in marketing channels. Intermediaries (also called channel members, resellers, and middlemen) negotiate with one another, buy and sell products, and facilitate the change of ownership between buyers and sellers in the course of moving the product from manufacturers into the hands of the final consumers.

Distribution channels may not be restricted to physical products alone. They may be just as important for moving a service from producer to consumer in certain sectors, since both direct and indirect channels may be used. Hotels, for example, may sell their services (typically rooms) directly or through travel agents, tour operators, airlines, tourist boards, centralized reservation systems, etc.

There have also been some innovations in the distribution of services. For example, there has been an increase in franchising and in rental services—the latter offering anything from televisions through tools. There has also been some evidence of service integration, with services linking together, particularly in the travel and tourism sectors. For example, links now exist between airlines, hotels and car rental services. In addition, there has been a significant increase in retail outlets for the service sector. Outlets such as estate agencies and building society offices are crowding out traditional grocers from major shopping areas.

Concept Check

1. Direct channel include _____, _____ and _____, and forms of electronic _____ like on-line shopping and shop-at-home television networks.

2. Most consumer products are sold through _____ similar to the other two alternatives: _____ and _____.

3. Hotels, for example, may sell their services directly or through _____, _____, _____, _____, centralized reservation systems, etc.

4. Marketing channels facilitate _____ through _____.

Group Discussion

1. What roles do the intermediaries play in the process of distribution?
2. In the city that you live, what organization can act as intermediary in the process of distribution?
3. What benefits will the intermediaries get out of the process of distribution?
4. What do the ordinary consumer get from the intermediaries?
5. Do you think the existence of intermediaries may impact the sales? How?

 Reading 2

Intermediaries

Intermediaries in a distribution channel negotiate with one another, facilitate the change of ownership between buyers and sellers, and physically move products from the manufacturer to the final consumer. The most prominent difference separating intermediaries is whether or not they take title to the product. Taking title means they own the merchandise and control the terms of the sale—e.g. price and delivery date. **Retailers** and **merchant wholesalers** are examples of intermediaries who take title to products in the marketing channel and resell them. Retailers are firms that sell mainly to consumers. Wholesalers are those organizations that facilitate the movement of products and services from the manufacturer to producers, resellers, governments, institutions and retailers. All merchant wholesalers take title to the goods they sell, and most of them operate one or more warehouses in which they receive goods, store them, and later reship them.

Other intermediaries do not take title to goods and services they market but do facilitate the exchange of ownership between sellers and buyers. **Agents and brokers** simply facilitate the sale of a product from producer to end-user by representing retailers, wholesalers, or manufacturers. Title reflects ownership, and ownership usually implies control. Unlike wholesalers, agents or brokers only facilitate sales and generally have little input into the terms of the sale. They do, however, get a free or commission based on sales volume.

Intermediaries perform several essential functions that make the flow of goods between producer and buyer possible. The three basic functions that intermediaries perform are summarized in Exhibit 9.2.

Types of function	Description
Transactional functions	***Contacting and promoting:*** contacting potential customers, promoting products, and soliciting orders ***Negotiating:*** determining how many goods or services to buy and sell, type of transportation to use, when to deliver and method and timing of payment ***Risk-taking:*** assuming the risk of owning inventory
Logistical functions	***Physically distributing:*** transporting and sorting goods to overcome temporal and spatial discrepancies ***Storing:*** maintaining inventories and protecting goods ***Sorting:*** overcoming discrepancies of quantity and assortment by ***Sorting out:*** breaking down a heterogeneous supply into separate homogeneous stocks ***Accumulation:*** combining similar stocks into a larger homogeneous supply ***Allocation:*** braking a homogeneous supply into smaller and smaller lots ***Assortment:*** combining products into collections or assortments the buyers want available at one place

Types of function	Description
Facilitating functions	***Researching:*** gathering information about other channel members and consumers ***Financing:*** extending credit and other financial services to facilitate the flow of goods through the channel to the final consumer

Exhibit 9.2 The Three Basic Functions

(Adapted from Charles W. Lamb, et al., *Marketing*, 6th Edition, South-Western Educational Publishing, 2002, Chapter 12.)

Notes

① Retailer: a channel intermediary that sells mainly to consumers 零售商

② Merchant wholesaler: an institution that buys goods from manufacturers and resells them to businesses, government agencies, and other wholesalers or retailers, and receives and takes title to goods, stores them in its own warehouses, and later ships them 批发商

③ Agents and brokers: wholesaling intermediaries who facilitate the sale of a product from producer to end user by representing retailers, wholesalers or manufacturers and do not take title to the product 代理商

④ Logistics: the process of strategically managing the efficient flow and storage of raw materials, in-process inventory, and finished goods from point of origin to point of consumption 物流

Concept Check

1. Intermediaries refer to _____.

2. The major difference separating intermediaries is _____.

3. What are merchant wholesalers?
_____

4. What is an agent?
_____

5. In your opinion, by what standards can people choose suitable intermediaries for delivering their products?
_____

 Activity 1

Where to Sell Product
—Paul Christ

A distribution system is only effective if customers can obtain the product. Consequently marketers must choose the approach that reaches customers in the most effective way. The most important decision with regard to reaching the target market is to determine the level of distribution coverage. There are three main levels of distribution coverage—mass, selective and exclusive coverage.

- Mass Coverage

The mass coverage (also known as intensive distribution) strategy attempts to distribute products widely in nearly all locations in which that type of product is sold. This level of distribution is only feasible for relatively low priced products that appeal to very large target markets (e.g., see consumer convenience products). A product such as Coca-Cola is a classic example since it is available in a wide variety of locations including grocery stores, convenience stores, vending machines, hotels and many, many more. With such a large number of locations selling the product the cost of distribution is extremely high and must be offset with very high sales volume.

- Selective Coverage

Under selective coverage the marketer deliberately seeks to limit the locations in which this type of product is sold. To the non-marketer it may seem strange that a marketer does not want to distribute their product in every possible location. However, the logic of this strategy is tied to the size and nature of the product's target market. Products with selective coverage appeal to smaller, more focused target markets (e.g. consumer shopping products) compared to the size of target markets for mass marketed products. Consequently, because the market size is smaller, the number of locations needed to support the distribution of the product is fewer.

- Exclusive Coverage

Some high-end products target very narrow markets that have a relatively small number of customers. These customers are often characterized as "discriminating" in their taste for products and seek to satisfy some of their needs with high-quality, though expensive products. Additionally, many buyers of high-end products require a high level of customer service from the channel member from whom they purchase. These characteristics of the target market may lead the marketer to sell their products through a very select or exclusive group of resellers. Another type of exclusive distribution may not involve high-end products but rather products only available in selected locations such as company-owned stores. While these products may or may not be higher priced compared to competitive products, the fact these are only available in company outlets gives exclusivity to the distribution.

Application

Have a discussion with your partner and try to figure out the approach (mass coverage, selective coverage, and exclusive coverage) that is suitable to deliver the following products.

Products	Intermediaries
Coca-cola	
Digital cameras	
New novels	
Fashionable clothes	
Automobiles	

 **Activity 2**

Why Are Intermediaries Needed?

As noted, distribution channels often require the assistance of others in order for the marketer to reach its target market. But why exactly does a company need others to help with the distribution of their product? Wouldn't a company that handles its own distribution functions be in a better position to exercise control over product sales and potentially earn higher profits? Also, doesn't the Internet make it much easier to distribute products thus lessening the need for others to be involved in selling a company's product?

While on the surface it may seem to make sense for a company to operate its own distribution channel (i.e. handling all aspects of distribution), there are many factors preventing companies from doing so. While companies can do without the assistance of certain channel members, some level of channel partnership is needed for many marketers. For example, marketers who are successful without utilizing resellers to sell their product (e.g., Dell Computers sells mostly through the Internet and not in retail stores) may still need assistance with certain parts of the distribution process (e.g., Dell uses parcel post shippers such as FedEx and UPS). In Dell's case creating their own transportation system makes little sense. Thus, by using shipping companies Dell is taking advantage of the transportation services offered to Dell and to Dell's customers.

Application

Have a discussion with your partner about the distribution of the following multinational corporations (MNCs), figure out how they distribute their products.

Companies	Distribution
Adidas	
Coca-cola	
Dell	
Apple	

Translation and Discussion (9)

Translate the following story and the questions into English, and then discuss the questions in English.

目前韩柳他们的销售管道采取的是自产自销的形式。他们在市中心最繁华的步行街设立总店，并在市区开了三家分店，生意都相当红火。三个人劲头十足，琢磨着要到另一个城市去开分店。

问题
1. 他们的服装店在选址的时候应该考虑哪些因素？
2. 如果他们真要进入另一个城市，在销售渠道方面有哪些选择？

Supplementary Material

When Do Conflicts Happen among Channel Members?

Inequitable channel relationships often lead to channel conflict, which is a clash of goals and methods among the members of a distribution channel. Often it arises because channel members refuse to keep pace with the times.

Sources of conflicts among channel members can be due to many different situations and factors. Often times, conflicts arise because channel members have conflicting goals. For instance, athletic footwear retailers want to sell as many shoes as possible in order to maximize profits, regardless of whether the shoes are manufactured by Nike, Adidas or Anta. But the Nike manufacturer wants a certain sales volume and market share in each market.

Conflicts can also arise when channel members fail to fulfill expectations of other channel members—for example, when a franchisee does not follow the rules set down by the franchiser, or when changes to warranty policy are not communicated to dealers, then conflicts may occur when dealers make repairs with the expectation that they will be reimbursed by the manufacturer. Further, ideological differences and different perceptions of reality can also cause conflicts among channel members. For example, retailers may believe "the customer is always right" and offer a very liberal return policy. Wholesalers and manufacturers may feel that people "try to get something for nothing" or don't follow product instructions carefully.

Conflicts within a channel can be either horizontal or vertical. Horizontal conflict occurs among channel members on the same level, such as two or more different wholesalers or two or more different retailers that handle the same manufacturer's brands. This type of channel conflict is found most often when manufacturers practice dual or multiple distribution strategies.

Many regard horizontal conflict as healthy competition. Much more serious is vertical conflict, which occurs between different levels in a marketing channel, most typically between the manufacturer and wholesaler and the manufacturer and retailer. Producer–versus–wholesaler conflict occurs when the producer chooses to bypass the wholesaler to deal directly with the consumer of retailer.

Application

1. Can you give an example of horizontal conflict and vertical conflict respectively?

2. In a small city with a population of 300,000, if there are more than 10 KFC stores, the competition between the franchisees will be too hard. In order to avoid this horizontal conflict, the franchiser KFC is very strict when choosing the applicants. You can visit https://baike.baidu.com/ to know more.

Supplementary Vocabulary

dealers 经销商
delivery 配送
distribution channel 分销管道
distribution policies 分销策略
exclusive dealing 独家销售
export agents 出口代理（商）
franchising 特许经营
integration 整合
merchandising 推销
multi-channel distribution 多渠道分销
physical distribution 实物分销
purchasing agent 采购代理
retail outlets 零售店
sales performance 销售表现 / 业绩
spokesperson 代言人

delivery time 交付时间
discount stores 折扣商店
distribution decisions 分销决策
distributors 分销商
exclusive distribution 独家分销
export jobbers 出口批发商
heavy buyer 大客户
mail-order retailers 邮购零售商
missionary selling 推销式销售
multilevel selling 多级销售
price-off promotions 降价促销
reseller 中间商
sales force 销售队伍
specialty retailers 专营零售商
title 所有权

manufacturers' export agents (MEA) 制造商出口代理
manufacturers' sales offices/branches 生产商的销售办事处 / 分支机构
distributor/store (private labels) brands 分销商 / 私有品牌

Unit 10

Advertising

After learning this unit, you should be able to answer the following questions.

- How to select advertising media?
- What is advertising?
- How to evaluate the effects of advertisements?
- How much should be used for advertising?

Advertising

Warm-up Activities

In what way do you get to know Jiaduobao (as shown in the picture below)? Do you think the advertisements of Jiaduobao have the desired effects? Why or why not?

(Picture from http://image.baidu.com)

 Reading 1

What Is Advertising?

With the trend toward a buyer's market today, modern marketing calls for more than just developing a good product, pricing it attractively, and making it available to target customers. Companies must also communicate with current and prospective customers. A company's total marketing communication mix, also called its promotion mix, consists of the blend of advertising, personal selling, sales promotion, public relations and any tools the company employs to achieve its business goals. The topic to discuss in this unit will be some major aspects of advertising.

Advertising, an important component in a company's promotion mix and the most widely employed and effective promotional means, can be defined in two aspects. In a broad sense, it is generally categorized as means and behaviors to inform the mass; while, in a narrow one, it can be defined as a marketing communication element that is persuasive, non-personal, paid for by an identified sponsor, and disseminated through mass channels of communication to promote the adoption of goods, services, persons, or ideas.

Advertising Message

Generally speaking, the influence of advertising on consumers is often explained by using the following hierarchy of effects, as shown in Exhibit 10.1. Of course, not every consumer consciously or subconsciously goes through a sequence of all the steps for all ads. Yet each stage of this hierarchy represents a specific goal for advertisers to pursue.

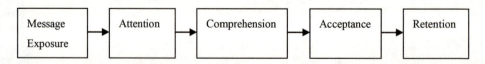

Exhibit 10.1

Marketers try to achieve the Message Exposure by placing ads in various kinds of advertising media, such as television, newspapers, magazines, radios and so on. Attention is the next step, during which process the ad stimulates consumers' interest. Yet only during the next stage, i.e., Message comprehension, does the consumer process and understand the ad. Then Message acceptance, must occur for the consumer to develop favorable attitudes about the advertised product or service and its subsequent purchase. Next, Message retention only occurs when the consumer stores ad information in long-term memory, which is significant for affecting later purchase decisions and behaviors.

As selective perception can occur at any stage, whether the consumer may go through all these stages and finally make the purchase action depends heavily on the message conveyed in the ad. Therefore, just as Gary Armstrong and Philip Kotler put it, "The message exposed should be just to gain and hold attention. Today's advertising messages must be better planned, more imaginative, more entertaining, and more rewarding to consumers."

The purpose of advertising is to get consumers to think about or react to the product or company in a certain way. People will react only if they believe that they will benefit from doing so. Thus, developing an effective message strategy begins with identifying the customer benefits that can be used as advertising appeals. Ideally, advertising message strategy will follow directly from the company's broader positioning strategy.

After deciding the primary benefit of the products, the advertiser must next develop a compelling creative concept, or "big idea", which will bring the message strategy to life in a distinctive and memorable way. At this stage, simple message ideas become great ad campaigns. Usually, a copywriter and art director will team up to generate many creative concepts, hoping that one of these concepts will turn out to be the big idea. The creative concept may emerge as a picture, a phrase, or a combination of the two. Moreover, for international advertising, marketers and ad agencies still need to recognize the influence of cultural diversity on advertising.

Advertising Objectives

Advertising objectives should be realistic, precise, and measurable, and consistent with the firm's overall marketing, and communications objectives. An advertising objective is a specific communication task to be accomplished with a specific target audience during a specific period of time.

Advertising objectives can be classified by their primary purpose: whether the aim is to inform, persuade, or remind, by which it can be categorized as informative advertising, persuasive advertising and reminder advertising. And according to its specific objectives, it can also be classified into the following types: to increase sales, to expand the market, to increase brand awareness, to communicate the company image.

Setting objectives enhances the firm's ability to evaluate the effectiveness of its advertising expenditures. Usually, marketers set broad advertising objectives to encourage consumers to try their products, to switch brands, to develop brand loyalty, and to increase per capita consumption. At the same time, they formulate intermediate and operational objectives, such as producing specific levels of consumer awareness, determining recall and recognition rates, encouraging consumers' knowledge of product attributes, and meeting consumers' interests, intentions, and so forth in particular markets.

 Reading 2

How to Budget and Evaluate an Advertisement?

Advertising Budget

After determining its advertising objectives, the company next sets its advertising budget for each product and market. Deciding how much to spend on advertising is of great importance and one of the hardest decisions for a company. Companies set budgets for various projects, while the following four approaches are frequently used to set the total budget for advertising: the affordable approach, the percentage-of-sales approach, the competitive-parity approach or competitor's expenditure approach, and the objective-and-task approach.

Affordable Approach Some companies set advertising budgets based on their subjective judgments, which is called the affordable approach. They set the promotion budget at the level they think the company can afford. Small companies often use this approach. By deducting the operating expenses and capital outlays from their total revenues in a specific period, usually one year, they get the amount they want to devote to advertising. Unfortunately, this approach does not place enough importance on advertising even though at the moment when advertising is crucial for the company to get awareness from their potential customers. This may lead to under-spending on advertising, which makes long-range market planning difficult.

Percentage-of-Sales Approach More commonly, companies use the percentage-of-sale approach. They use some percentage of previous year's sales or this year's expected sales (e.g. Three percent) to set advertising budgets for the current year, or some of them may set a percentage of the unit sales price. This approach is simple to use and helps marketers think through the relationships between promotion spending, selling price, and profit per unit. However, this approach is hard to justify. Budget in this way is based on availability of funds rather than on opportunities. It may prevent the increased spending sometimes needed to turn around falling sales, because the budget varies with year-to-year sales, long-range planning is difficult. Finally, this approach cannot provide a specific percentage for advertising, just what was done in the past or what competitors are doing now.

Competitive-parity Approach   Some other companies may base their advertising budget on competitor's expenditures. They match the competition in the market, set an amount above or equal to the competition. Marketers who choose this advertising budget approach either believe that competitors' budgets represent the collective wisdom of the industry or that spending what competitors spend helps prevent promotion wars. However, companies differ greatly from each other, and each has its own promotion needs and there is no evidence that this kind of budget can prevent promotion wars.

Objective-and-Task Approach   As marketers have realized the above-mentioned disadvantages of the previous three approaches, they wish to set advertising budgets at levels appropriate to stimulate their sales. Thus, many marketers employ the objective-and-task approach, which helps them set budgets so that advertising meets organization goals more closely. Usually, the company defines a specific goal (e.g. "fifty percent awareness of our new product by consumers within four months"), and then works together with their advertising agencies, if any, to design tasks (numbers of ad to show, the media to use, and so forth) to reach the goal. This approach forces management to spell out its assumptions about the relationship between the amount spent and promotion results. Yet it is also the most difficult method to use, as it is hard to figure out which specific tasks will achieve specific goals.

No matter what approach is employed, setting the advertising budget is not easy. Therefore, marketers must consider costs, such as message design and media costs. When they set their advertising budget, they must take a long-run perspective, continuously monitoring results and making changes when necessary to ensure that their advertising budgets and programs match their corporate goals and strategies.

Advertising Evaluation

To achieve better effects in future advertising campaigns, marketers should regularly evaluate the effect of their past or current advertising. Most companies tend to evaluate the communication effects and the sales effects of advertising. For the communication effects, copy testing usually proves to be an effective method. Before the ad is placed, the advertiser can show it to consumers, ask how they like it, and measure recall or attitude changes resulting from it. After the ad is run, the advertiser can measure how the ad affects consumer recall or product awareness, knowledge, and preference.

As compared with the communication effects, sales effects is harder to measure, as sales are affected by many factors besides advertising, such as product features, price, and availability. One possible way to measure the sales effect of advertising is to compare past sales with past advertising expenditures. Another way is through experiments. Marketers could vary the amount they spend on advertising in different market areas and measure the differences in the resulting sales levels. For example, they can spend the normal amount in one market area, half in another, and twice in a third area. If the three market areas are similar, and if all other marketing efforts in the area are the same, differences in sales in the three areas could be related to advertising level. More complex experiments could be designed to include other variables, such as difference in the ads or media used.

(Adapted from Gary Armstrong & Philip Kotler, *Marketing: An Introduction*, Prentice-Hall, Inc., 2000, Chapter12.)

Activity 1

Mengniu's Great Success

In the July of 1999, when Mengniu Dairy (Group) Co., Ltd was founded, its registered capital was only around 10 million RMB, ranked No.119 in China dairy enterprises. However, by the end of 2007, its sales revenue had reached 21.3 billion RMB, with a Compound Annual Growth Rate (CAGR) of 121% which made Mengniu the first dairy company that exceeded 20 billion RMB in sales revenue in China; the sales of UHT (Ultra High Temperature Treated) milk had ranked No.1 in the world and that of liquid milk, yogurt and ice cream ranked No.1 in China; the export volume and the number of regions exported had also ranked No.1 in China.

Undoubtedly, many factors attribute to Mengniu's great achievements, among which, advertising plays an indispensable role which can be proved by the following facts. In the CCTV's inviting public bidding for its advertising sponsors in the year 2004, Mengniu ranked No.1 among dairy industry enterprises with an amount of 310 million RMB spent on advertising in CCTV only.

Questions

Now, with reference to the information about Advertising Message in Reading 1 and Advertising Budget in Reading 2, discuss the following questions in groups.

(Pictures from http://image.baidu.com)

1. What message does each of these advertisements convey to you? While designing advertising messages, what should marketers bear in mind?

2. What objectives does each of the advertisements aim at?

3. Mengniu's advertising penetrates almost every corner in the country, and the company spends a lot on advertising. In the year 2004, Mengniu spent 374 million RMB on advertising, accounting for 8.9% of its total sales volumes. Why do you think Mengniu budgets so much for advertising?

 Activity 2

JDB's Great Success by Sponsoring *Voice of China*

The JDB (Jiaduobao) Group is a Hongkong-based, large scale enterprise that focuses its business in the production and sales of specialized beverages. It was founded in 1995, while it was not until 2012, that the Group became popular among every household in China because of its exclusive sponsoring of *The Voice of China*（中国好声音）. In 2012, the Group spent only 60 million RMB for the advertising activity, while with the increasing popularity of *The Voice of China*, its exclusive sponsoring price has risen to 200 million RMB, more than three times of the price of the previous year, but the JDB Group still bid for it and won the competitive bidding in the end.

Group Discussion

Discuss in groups this advertising activity of the JDB Group according to the ideas you have got from the reading materials. You may focus on the advertising message, advertising objectives, advertising budget, or the selection of media and so on.

Activity 3

Translation and Discussion (10)

Translate the following story and the questions into English, and then discuss the questions in English.

服装店的口碑主要靠顾客的口口相传，店面的装修风格和店内的服装摆设也是吸引顾客的重要因素。随着市场的扩大，韩柳他们三人寻思着是否要适当地做些广告。

问题
1. 你觉得他们有必要做广告吗？
2. 如果要做广告，选择什么样的媒介比较好呢？

Supplementary Material

How to Select Appropriate Media?

Advertising media planning involves decisions on the following aspects: ① deciding on reach, frequency, and impact; ② choosing among major media types (television, magazines etc.); ③ selecting specific media vehicles (specific television programs, magazines etc.); and ④ deciding on media timing.

Deciding on Reach, Frequency and Impact To select media, the advertiser must decide what reach and frequency are needed to achieve objectives. Reach is a measure of the percentage of people who are exposed to the ad campaign in a specific period of time. Frequency is a measure of how many times the average person in the target market is exposed to the message. Moreover, marketers still have to take the desired media impact into consideration, i.e. which media type can best achieve the effect they expect. Usually, the more reach, frequency and impact the advertiser seeks, the higher the advertising budget will have to be.

Choosing among major media types As each may be different in the reach, frequency and impact for specific products or services, marketers have to choose, according to the characteristics of their products, the most appropriate one of the major media types: newspaper, television, direct mail, radio, magazine, outdoor and Internet. The advantages and limitations of these media types have been classified in Exhibit 10.2.

Medium	Advantages	Limitations
Newspaper	flexibility; timelines; good local market coverage; broad acceptability; high believability	short life; poor reproduction quality; small pass–along audience
Television	good mass–market coverage; low cost per exposure; combining sight, sound, and motion; appealing to the senses	high absolute costs; high clutter; fleeting exposure; less audience selectivity
Direct Mail	high audience selectivity; flexibility; no ad competition within the same medium; allows personalization	relatively high cost per exposure; "junk mail" image
Radio	good local acceptance; high geographic and demographic selectivity; low cost	audio only; fleeting exposure; low attention ("the half–heard" medium); fragmented audiences
Magazine	high geographic and demographic selectivity; credibility and prestige; high quality reproduction; long life and good pass–along readership	long ad–purchase lead time; high cost; no guarantee of position
Outdoor	flexibility; high repeat exposure; low cost; low message competition; good positional selectivity	little audience selectivity; creative limitations
On–line	high selectivity; low cost; immediacy; interactive capability	small, demographically skewed audience; relatively low impact; audience controls exposure

Exhibit 10.2 The Advantages and Limitations of Different Media Types

With these advantages and limitations of different media types in mind, media planners still consider many factors when choosing among the major media. In general, what they concerned most is the media habits of target consumers, the nature of the product, different type of messages and cost. To achieve the best effect, marketers are increasingly turning to alternative media, ranging from cable TV and outdoor advertising to parking meters and shopping carts, which cost less and target more effectively.

Selecting Specific Media Vehicles The media then must choose the best media vehicles, specific media within each general media type. For example, television vehicles include different types of programs and there are different types of magazines and radio programs as well. Generally speaking, in selecting media vehicles, the media planner must balance media cost measures against several media impact factors. First, the media vehicle's audience quality is of great importance. For a baby lotion advertisement, for example, new parents magazine would have a high-exposure value. Second, audience attention is crucial as well. Readers of some magazines or newspapers may pay more attention to ads than some others do. Third, the editorial quality should also be considered. Some media vehicles are more believable and prestigious than others.

Deciding On Media Timing About media selection, marketers must take media timing into consideration as well, that is to say, they have to decide the best advertising over the course of a year. Some companies choose the timing according to the slack or peak selling seasons of their products in a specific area.

Next, marketers have to choose the pattern of the ads. Continuity means scheduling ads evenly while pulsing means scheduling ads unevenly within a given period. Thus, 52 ads could either be arranged at one per week or pulsed in several bursts only during a year.

Today, advanced technology such as new computer software applications has had a substantial impact on the media planning, which helps advertisers to make better decisions about which mix of networks, programs, and time slots will yield the highest reach per ad dollar.

(Adapted from Gary Armstrong & Philip Kotler, *Marketing: An Introduction*, Prentice-Hall, Inc., 2000,Chapter12.)

Questions

1. What factors are involved in advertising media planning?
2. What should be considered as far as the selecting of specific media vehicles is concerned?

Unit 11

Sales Promotion

After learning this unit, you should be able to answer the following questions.

- What are the limitations of sales promotion?
- What is sales promotion?
- What tools can be used for sales promotion?
- What objectives does sales promotion aim at?
- What are the favorable factors for the rapid growth of sales promotion?

Warm-up Activities

If advertising and personal selling offer reasons to buy a product or service, sales promotion offers reasons to buy now.

What's your understanding of the above saying? How important do you think sales promotion is to an organization? What tools do you know that can be used in sales promotion?

 Reading 1

What Is Sales Promotion?

To seek better business effects, marketers often try to utilize all forms of marketing combinations to grow their business. Thus, they usually think of sales promotion as a supplement to other elements of the communication mix. Sales promotion refers to short-term incentives to encourage the purchase or sale of a product or service. A unique characteristic of sales promotion is that it offers an incentive for action. In contrast to many forms of advertising, sales promotion is oriented towards achieving short-term results, so we can tell while advertising and personal selling offer reasons to buy a product or service, sales promotion offers reasons to buy now. Examples of sales promotion are found everywhere. A consumer might receive a rebate for making a purchase, for instance, or a retailer may be offered an allowance for purchasing a specific quantity of a product, or an executive may buy a new laptop computer and get a free carrying case.

Sales promotion can be classified in two categories—consumer sales promotion and trade sales promotion, as it can be directed at either the customer, sales staff, or distribution channel members (such as retailers). Sales promotion targeted at the consumer is called **consumer sales promotion** and that targeted at retailers and wholesale is called **trade sales promotion**.

Rapid Growth of Sales Promotion

Various sales promotion techniques are used by many organizations, they are targeted towards different types of people, ranging from end users, retailers and wholesalers to members of the sales force. But what has motivated the growth of sales promotion in recent years? Changes in the marketing environment—consumers' attitudes, greater pressure product managers to increase sales, more competition the company faces, the declining effect of advertising, and the changes in retailing—are favorable for the development of sales promotion.

First, consumers have become more deal oriented. Shoppers get a lot of satisfaction from getting a good deal and they are used to special sales, rebates, and other forms of sales promotion. As consumers expect more deals, retailers also regard sales promotion as necessary stimulus to increase, or even maintain, sales in today's competitive environment and they in turn demand more deals from manufacturers.

Second, inside the company, there is greater pressure for product managers to increase the sales of their products and different kinds of sales promotion are considered as effective measures for the situation.

Third, the company faces more competition within the same scope of the business and competing brands are so similar that it is hard for consumers to differentiate. Thus, sales promotion is employed by many companies to help consumers to differentiate their products from those of their competitors.

Moreover, because of rising costs, media clutter, legal restraint and other unfavorable factors, the effect of advertising has declined. More marketers have turned to sales promotion to make their products tried by more consumers and increase the awareness of their products among existing customers.

Finally, the increased retail power contributes a lot to sales promotion as well. Huge retailers such as Wal-Mart and Carrefour have achieved great success because of their immense purchasing power. Sales promotion directed at both retailers and consumers make the manufacturers' products more appealing. Furthermore, with more power, they have tried to increase sales of their own private brand products by giving more discounts to their customers, which often helps push sales promotion further ahead.

Sales Promotion Objectives

Though all sales promotion aims at a common goal—to affect the present or future behaviors of consumers, consumer sales promotion and trade sales promotion present some different specific objectives. Marketers may use sales promotions to increase short-term sales or to help long-term market share. The objectives for consumer promotion include the following factors: to get consumers to try a product, to encourage people to buy more than they would need, to encourage repeat purchase among existing customers, to weaken or even invalidate the promotions of other brands, to attract buyers to some complementary products while buying a basic one or to stimulate impulse purchasing by using special feature displays on the shopping site.

Meanwhile, objectives for trade promotion include gaining new retailers or maintaining existing ones; to influence retailers to promote the product; to influence retailers to offer a price discount and thus increasing the sales; to get retailers to carry new items and more inventories, and to defend against competitors.

Sales promotion is usually used together with advertising or personal selling. Consumer promotions must usually be advertised thus adding excitement and pulling power to ads.

In general, sales promotions should be consumer relationship building rather than creating only short-term sales or temporary brand switching. They should help to reinforce the product's position and build long-term relationships with customers.

 Reading 2

What Tools Can Be Used for Sales Promotion?

As consumer sales promotion and trade sales promotion carry different specific objectives, different tools or techniques tend to be used to realize their objectives as well.

Consumer Promotion Tools/Techniques

First, the main tools for consumer promotion include price deals, samples, coupons, cash refunds, advertising specialties, premiums, patronage rewards, point-of-purchase displays and demonstrations, contest, sweepstakes and games.

Price Deals A price deal is a temporary reduction in the price of a product. There are two types of price deals: cents-off deals and price-pack deals. The former offers a brand at less than the regular price while the latter offers consumers something extra through the packaging itself.

Samples A sample is a small size of a product made available to potential buyers. Some samples are often free of charge, or the company just charges a small amount to offset its cost. Marketers find sampling very useful for new brands with features that are difficult to describe adequately through advertising. The sample may be distributed door-to-door, sent by mail, handed out in a store, at trade shows, movies, special events or attached to another product. Sometimes, samples are combined into sample packs, which can then be used to promote other products and services. Sampling is the most effective, but also the most expensive way to introduce a new product, so marketers must determine the most cost-effective manner of distribution.

Coupons Coupons are printed certificates giving their bearers a stated price reduction or special value on a specific product, generally for a specific period of time. Coupons may be distributed in several ways. Coupons can stimulate sales of a mature brand and are particularly useful in encouraging new-product trials. Coupons may be distributed through several ways. The most popular one is through the mail and freestanding inserts or ads in newspapers and magazines. Nowadays, however, they are increasingly distributed via shelf dispensers at the point of sale, by electronic point-of-sale coupon printers, or through the Internet.

Cash Refunds Cash refunds (also called rebates) refer to cash sent back to buyers for purchasing a product. They are like coupons except that the rebate occurs after the purchase rather than at the retail outlet. Consumers send a rebate form, the purchase receipt, or some proof of purchase to the manufacturer within a certain period. As consumers may forget to send for the rebate or run out of time, it is not as convenient as coupons, but rebates still serve several functions. They attract customers, particularly price-conscious buyers for their economic appeal. They also offer a good way to reduce the perceived risk in trying a new brand, as a lower price represents less risk to most customers. Rebates also encourage increased consumption.

Advertising Specialties (also called promotional gifts) Advertising specialties are items of useful or interesting merchandise given away free of charge and typically carrying an imprinted name or message. These items are often low in cost. The typical ones can be balloons, pens, calendars, yardsticks, coffee mugs, notebooks, key rings, T-shirts, caps, nail files, shopping bags and so on. Advertising specialties can reinforce other advertising media to strengthen the message. A unique specialty advertising item can attract interest among target audience members and perhaps stimulate action. Poor-quality merchandise, however, may turn against the marketers' good will.

Patronage Rewards Patronage rewards are cash or other awards offered for the regular use of a certain company's products or services. For example, some airlines offer frequent-flier plans, awarding points for miles traveled that can be turned in for free airline trips. And some hotels such as 7-Day Inn offers frequent-use awards—for every 7 nights, customers receive a free night in the hotel.

Point-of-purchase Displays and Demonstrations Point-of-purchase displays and demonstrations include displays and demonstrations that take place at the point of purchase or sale. These displays aim at attracting more consumers' attention to the products.

Contest, Sweepstakes and Games Contest, sweepstakes and games give consumers the chance to win something, such as cash, trips, or goods, by luck or through extra effort. A contest offers prizes based on the skill of contestants. Participants must use a skill or some ability to address a specified problem to qualify for a prize. A sweepstakes offers prizes based on a chance drawing of participants' name. Sweepstakes have strong appeal because they are easier to enter and take less time than contest and games. A game presents consumers with something—bingo numbers, missing letters—every time they buy, which may or may not help them win a prize. Games are similar to sweepstakes, but they cover a longer period.

Trade Promotion Tools/Techniques

More sales promotion dollars are directed to retailers and wholesalers than to consumers, and marketers employ lots of techniques for trade sales promotion. These techniques can be applied independently or in combinations. Many of the techniques used for consumer promotion (such as contests, rebates, and displays) can also be used as trade promotions. Some frequently used trade sales promotion techniques include trade allowance, trade shows, dealer loaders, training programs and push money.

Trade Allowances Trade allowances are short-term special allowances, discounts, or deals granted to retailers as an incentive to stock, feature, or in some way participate in the cooperative promotion of a product. An advertising allowance compensates retailers for advertising the product. A display allowance compensates them for using special displays. A manufacturer usually offers a buying allowance to increase the size of the retailers' order.

Trade Shows A trade show is a periodic, semipublic event sponsored by trade, professional, and industrial associations at which suppliers rent booths to display products and provide information to potential buyers. They are greatly influential in many markets in the world, including the US, Europe, the Middle East, Africa, Asia, and Latin America. For example, a quarter of the international trade contracts in China are signed during the two sessions of the Chinese Export Commodities Fair in Guangzhou.

Training Programs Some manufacturers sponsor or pay for training programs for customer employees. Marketers may also provide training on a number of other topics, including retail and wholesale management procedures, safety issues, or current technical developments in an industrial field. Training programs are expensive, and results are often hard to measure. Moreover, to be effective, training should be continual, or at least periodically reinforced, thus adding to the expense. Even though it is expensive, training can build productive relationships with customers.

Push Money (also called Spiffs) Push money is what a manufacturer pays to retail salespeople to encourage them to promote its products over competitive brands. Push money may also be used to encourage the retail sale of specific products in the manufacturer's line. This extra incentive helps to get the manufacturer's brand special representation or favored treatment. However, the retail salespeople's extra enthusiasm for the manufacturer's product may decline or even stop once the spiffs is no longer in function.

 Activity 1

The Advantages and Disadvantages of Sales Promotion

You may be very familiar with the picture above, which is a promotional advertisement of a supermarket for a short period (about 10 days). Combine the information about the sales promotion in Reading 1 and the information in the Supplementary Reading part of this unit, discuss the following questions in groups.

1. What advantages and disadvantages/limitations does this kind of promotional campaigns bear?

2. Suppose you are a manager in such a supermarket, what measures will you use to reduce the negative effects brought on by such a promotion?

Activity 2

The following are some cases of sales promotion. Discuss in groups to define what tool/tools is/are used in each case and what are the advantages and disadvantages of each tool.

Item 1 Item 2

Item 3 Item 4

Item 5

(Pictures from http://image.baidu.com)

Activity 3

Translation and Discussion (11)

Translate the following story and the questions into English, and then discuss the questions in English.

虽然自己的服装设计得很好，质量也上乘，但是现在市场竞争激烈，要想保住老顾客，吸引新顾客，就得好好动动脑筋。

问题
1. 对于服装店的促销，你有什么好主意？
2. 打折和降价促销有区别吗？为什么？

Supplementary Material

What Are the Limitations of Sales Promotion?

Although sales promotion can accomplish a variety of objectives, there are certain things it cannot do. Sales promotion can help boost sales, but it cannot reverse a genuine declining sales trend. If sales are slipping, marketers should evaluate and perhaps change the product's marketing strategy. Attempting to use sales promotion as a quick fix may temporarily postpone worsening of the problem, but it cannot eliminate it.

Similarly, marketers cannot reasonably expect sales promotion to convert rejection of an inferior product into acceptance. Consumers judge a product on whether it satisfies their needs.

Products that do not meet consumers' needs naturally fade from the market over the course of time.

Beyond its inability to improve a brand's image, sales promotion may even weaken the brand image. As a sales promotion develops a life of its own, perceived product differentiation may be blurred; consumers come to see the deal as more important than any other real or perceived brand difference. In essence, buyers reach a point at which they fail to see any differences among brands, and the marketer has unwittingly created short-run price-oriented behavior. In the soft-drink market, for instance, many consumers see Coca-Cola and Pepsi-Cola as interchangeable and decide which of the two they will purchase primarily on the basis of price (which is the better deal?).

Sales promotion, far more than other marketing activities, has also been blamed for encouraging competitive retaliation. Promotion can be developed quickly, and one company can respond to a competitor's sales promotion with its own. Quick response may stave off the potential of sales lost to the competitor's promotion. Although a promotion battle benefits consumers, two firms that compete head-to-head often both lose profits. Other forms of marketing communications are less likely to evoke such quick retaliatory efforts.

Sales promotion can result in manufacturers gaining short-term volume but sacrificing profit. Special incentives and deals promote forward buying, both among distributors and consumers. That is, people buy more than they need at the deal price. They purchase enough to carry them to the next deal, when once again they can stock up at low price. Thus, the manufacturer may sell more at the expense of less profit.

(Adapted from William O., Bearden et al., *Marketing: Principles & Perspectives*, 2nd Edition, McGraw-Hill, 2001, p. 464)

Questions

1. What are the limitations of Sales Promotion?

2. Suppose you are the manager of a supermarket, how do you attract your customers by offering goods of value for money while avoiding the limitations of sales promotion to the best of your abilities?

Unit 12

Public Relations

After learning this unit, you should be able to answer the following questions.

- What are the major public relations tools?
- What is public relations?
- **Public Relations**
- What is the difference between public relations and advertising?
- What does a public relations department do?

 Warm-up

How does the cover of this book——*The Fall of Advertising & the Rise of PR*（《公关第一，广告第二》）strike you? In what way do you think Public Relations affects the business of an enterprise?

What Does a Public Relations Department Do?

The Definition of Public Relations(PR)

Ivy Lee and Edward Louis Bernays established the first definition of public relations in the early 1900s as "a management function, which tabulates public attitudes, defines the policies, procedures, and interests of an organization... followed by executing a program of action to earn public understanding and acceptance."

In August 1978, the World Assembly of Public Relations Associations defined the field as "the art and social science of analyzing trends, predicting their consequences, counseling organizational leaders, and implementing planned programs of action, which will serve both the organization and the public interest."

Public Relations Society of America, a professional trade association, defined public relations in 1982 as: "Public relations helps an organization and its publics adapt mutually to each other."

In 2011 and 2012, the PRSA developed a crowd-sourced definition: "Public relations is a strategic communication process that builds mutually beneficial relationships between organizations and their publics."

Public relations can also be defined as the practice of managing communication between an organization and its publics.

As Armstrong (2000) put it, public relations is a major mass-promotion tool to build good relations with the company's or organization's various publics by obtaining favorable publicity, building up a good corporate or organization image, and handling or heading off unfavorable rumors, stories, and events. Specifically, public relation refers to any form of non-paid commercially significant news or editorial comment about ideas, products, or institutions. Newspapers, television or radio stations, or magazines usually convey such information.

Negative public relations

Negative public relations, also called dark public relations (DPR) and in some earlier writing "Black PR", is a process of destroying the target's reputation and/or corporate identity. The objective in DPR is to discredit someone else, who may pose a threat to the client's business or be a political rival. DPR may rely on IT security, industrial espionage, social engineering and competitive intelligence. Common techniques include using dirty secrets from the target, producing misleading facts to fool a competitor. Some claim that negative public relations may be highly moral and beneficial for the general public since threat of losing the reputation may be disciplining for companies, organizations and individuals. Apart from this, negative public relations helps to expose legitimate claims against one.

The Role of a Public Relations Department

Public relations can have strong impact on public awareness at a much lower cost than advertising. Moreover, the major advantage of public relations, other than its free or lower cost aspect, is that the public generally perceives the information more positively than what they perceive in advertising, as people perceive the information more as impartial, thus the results or public relations can sometimes be spectacular.

Despite its potential strengths, public relation is often described as a marketing stepchild because of its limited and scattered use. More often than not, public relations department is usually located at corporate headquarters of large or multinational companies. Moreover, the staffs in the public relations department are so busy dealing with various publics—stockholders, employees, legislators, city officials—that public relations programs to support product marketing objectives may be ignored. That is why marketing managers and public relations practitioners do not always communicate smoothly, because public relations practitioners concern more about communications, while marketing managers are usually more interested in how advertising and public relations affected sales and profits.

Fortunately, the situation has changed nowadays, for most companies have realized that public relations is more than to inform the press of such information as a product release but also of research, counseling, planning and communications.

Crisis management/communication is another important part of PR.

Crisis management/communication is sometimes considered a sub-specialty of the public relations profession that is designed to protect and defend an individual, company, or organization facing a public challenge to its reputation. These challenges may come in the form of an investigation from a government agency, a criminal allegation, a media inquiry, a shareholders lawsuit, a violation of environmental regulations, or any of a number of other scenarios involving the legal, ethical, or financial standing of the entity.

Crisis management/communication can include crafting statements, known as "messages", often tested by research and polling. A rapid response capability—pioneered by the 1992 Clinton-Gore campaign operatives and refined during Bill Clinton's eight years under attack by his political adversaries while in the White House, has also become an essential element of crisis communication. Additional tactics may include proactive media outreach to get messages and context to the media, identifying and recruiting credible third-party allies who can attest to the company's side of the story, and striking first, not waiting to be hit.

The aim of crisis management/communication in this context is to assist organizations to achieve continuity of critical business processes and information flows under crisis, disaster or event driven circumstances.

In 2008, when melamine (三聚氰胺) was found in milk powder produced by some well-known companies in China, the PR departments of these companies tried quite different ways to prevent the negative effects on their sales. Yili (伊利) and Mengniu (蒙牛), for example, immediately responded to the media and promised to take back and refund for all their sold defective products and assured consumers of the safety of their new products.

Nowadays, PR is widely used not only by marketers in companies, but also by officials or politicians in public affair organizations. To be more specific, corporations use marketing public relations (MPR) to convey information about their products or services to their potential customers. And corporations also use public-relations as a vehicle to reach legislators and other politicians, seeking a favorable investing environment or reduction of tax and other favorable treatments which may be crucial for the development of their companies. Meanwhile, politicians also use public relations to attract votes and raise money in support of their successful election. Afterwards efforts in public relations will sustain support for their service while in office or even with an eye to the next election.

 Reading 2

What Are the Major Public Relations Tools?

Public relations is used to promote products, people, places, ideas, activities, organizations, and even nations. Trade associations have used public relations to rebuild interest in declining commodities. Generally, for different purposes, public relations professionals use several tools.

One of the major tools is news. Public relations professionals find or create favorable news about the company and its products or people. The news stories may occur naturally or the PR people can plan some events or activities that would create news. The speeches of PR representatives can also generate awareness for the products or services for an organization. However, such speeches may either build or hurt the company's image, thus they should be conducted with care.

Moreover, PR practitioners also prepare written or audiovisual materials to reach and influence the target market. Such materials range from annual reports, brochures, articles and company newsletters and magazines to films, slide-and-sound programs, video-and audiocassettes and so forth. Moreover, PR practitioners also try to instantly impress their target publics with corporate identity materials by constantly presenting distinctive and memorable logos, stationery, business cards, buildings, company cars or trucks and so on.

In addition, special events can be regarded as another widely used PR tool. These special events include news conferences, press tours, grand openings, and firework displays or even laser shows, hot-air balloon releases, multimedia presentations and star-studded activities, or educational programs designed to reach and interest target publics.

In the information age, however, most companies place great emphasis on the development of distinctive corporate Web sites. The more distinctive and effective the design of Web sites, the more click rates, which in turn will give the corporation more publicity. Company' Web sites can especially serve as an effective PR vehicle when an emergency occurs, for it is ideal when handling crisis situations. For example, when several bottles of Odwalla apple juice sold on the West coast of the States were found to contain Escherichia coli bacteria（大肠杆菌）, the company initiated a massive product recall. Within only three hours, it set up a Web site laden with information about the crisis and Odwalla's response. Company staff also used the Internet to look for newsgroups discussing Odwalla and posted links to the site.

Notes

① Odwalla: 美国果汁生产商，2001年被可口可乐公司收购，现为可口可乐全资子公司。

② The definitions of PR are adapted from http://en.wikipedia.org/wiki/Public_relations

and Gary Armstrong & Philip Kotler, *Marketing: An Introduction*, Prentice-Hall, Inc.,2000.

 **Activity 1**

The Difference between Advertising and Public Relations

Usually, the key concern of advertisers is to design advertisements, prepare advertising messages and buy time or space from different media. Their objective is to encourage or persuade their potential customers to purchase their products or services, whereas public relations specialists aim at communicating with various stakeholders, managing the organization's image and reputation, and creating positive public attitudes (goodwill towards the organization). Public relations tend to take a longer, broader view of the importance of image and reputation as a corporate competitive asset and address more target audiences.

In addition, advertising focuses on products, i.e. the sales of products whereas public relations is mostly concerned about the organization and its corporate image. Another distinctive difference between them is that public relations can have a strong impact on public awareness at a much lower cost than advertising. Moreover, the major advantage of public relations is that public relations usually enjoys higher credibility because people generally perceive the information as more impartial compared with that of advertising.

Application

Suppose you are the head of the PR department of a dairy company, what will your department do when you face the following situations?

Situation 1: Your company's annual report reveals that the sales volume of this year went down by 5% compared with that of last year, and the market survey proves that most of your customers turned to other brands because they expected more customer-friendly activities which they can receive from your competitors.

Situation 2: You just noticed, in a local newspaper, an article which reported that some ingredients in your products are harmful to people's health if taken regularly. Actually, your products do not contain that kind of ingredients at all.

Activity 2

In the year 2008, the Orleans Toast Chicken Wing, a product of Kentucky Fried Chicken (KFC), was inspected and found to contain Sudan red I (苏丹红I号) which is considered to be a carcinogen (致癌物质). KFC immediately stopped the sales of the food and apologized to the public on the media. They dealt with the crisis professionally and gained good feedback. Now New Orleans Toast Chicken Wing remains one of the best selling KFC products.

However, almost at the same time, Nestle Milk Powder was inspected and found to contain excessive iodine, which is harmful to people's health especially the infants' and children's. Nestle Corporation solved the problem step by step.

At first, it wanted to hide the facts and refused to apologize to the public, and when they eventually apologized they did not offer a refund. In the end, they offered a refund under public pressure. Due to their approach, they suffered huge losses, not only in sales, but also customer loyalty to the brand.

Questions

1. Both companies reacted to the problem immediately, why did they get quite different results after similar events?

2. If you were head of the PR department of Nestle, how would you deal with the problem? And why do you choose to solve the problem in that way?

 Activity 3

Translation and Discussion (12)

Translate the following story and the questions into English, and then discuss the questions in English.

服装店所在的街道经常有街委会的工作人员到店里发放一些号召给灾区捐款捐物的宣传资料。开始的时候他们都捐一些，后来由于各种捐款名目繁多，他们便开始烦起来，有时候甚至会拒绝。现在街委会的人员对他们的店颇有微词。

问题

1. 捐款事件会对他们店的生意造成影响吗？
2. 你认为他们应该如何处理好这种公共关系呢？

Supplementary Material

The Importance of Public Relations

—*Suan Jan*

Public relations is fundamentally the art and science of establishing relationships between an organization and its key audiences. Public relations plays a key role in helping business industries create strong relationships with customers.

Public relations involves supervising and assessing public attitudes, and maintaining mutual relations and understanding between an organization and its public. The function of public relations is to improve channels of communication and to institute new ways of setting up a two-way flow of information and understanding.

Public relations is effective in helping: Corporations convey information about their products or services to potential customers; Corporations reach local government and legislators; Politicians attract votes and raise money, and craft their public image and legacy; Non-profit organizations, including schools, hospitals, social service agencies etc. boost support of their programs such as awareness programs, fund-raising programs, and to increase patronage of their services.

Public relations in present times employs diverse techniques such as opinion polling and focus groups to evaluate public opinion, combined with a variety of high-tech techniques for distributing information on behalf of their clients, including the Internet, satellite feeds, broadcast faxes, and database-driven phone banks.

As public image is important to all organizations and prominent personalities, the role of a public relations specialist becomes pertinent in crisis situations. Public relations agencies provide important and timely transmission of information that helps save the face of the organization. In the words of the Public Relations Society of America (PRSA), "Public relations helps an organization and its public adapt mutually to one another."

Experienced public relations agencies have formulation press releases into which they can plug the company news, as well as a targeted list of publications for their industry. Truly good public relations agencies generally have a good working relationship with key reporters, boosting their chances of getting coverage. Some public relations agencies deal only with large, established clients, while smaller boutique public relations agencies specialize in certain areas.

At present public relations as a career option exists in private companies or government institutions that actively market their product, service and facilities. Public relations training courses are widespread in educational institutions. According to the U.S. Bureau of Labor Statistics, there were 122,000 public relations specialists in the United States in 1998 and approximately 485,000 advertising, marketing, and public relations managers working in all industries.

Most public relations practitioners are recruited from the ranks of journalism. Public relations officers are highly trained professionals with expertise and knowledge in many areas, for example, shareholder management during a crisis, the evolving role of the in-house public relations professional, account management skills for public relations, an introduction to financial public relations, an introduction to consumer public relations, an introduction to public relations software and etc.

Questions

1. How important is public relations to a business?
2. Are you willing to be a PR consultant in the future? Why/Why not?

Unit 13

Personal Selling

After learning this unit, you will be able to answer the following questions.

- In what way can you talk to your customers?
- What is personal selling?
- Personal Selling
- What are the steps in the selling process?
- What makes a good salesperson?

 Warm-up

Salespeople are made, not born. For most salespeople, sales excellence does not just come naturally.

—Linda Richardson

Do you agree with the above quote? In which aspects do you think that a salesperson should be trained?

 Reading 1

What Is Personal Selling?

Personal selling is a promotional method in which one party (e.g., a salesperson) uses skills and techniques for building personal relationships with another party (e.g., those involved in a purchase decision) that results in both parties obtaining value. In most cases the "value" for the salesperson is realized through the financial rewards of the sale while the customer's "value" is realized from the benefits obtained by consuming the product.

Personal selling is one of the oldest forms of promotion, and the role of personal selling can vary from one company to another. Some firms have no salespeople at all—for example, organizations that sell only through mailorder, catalogues or through manufacturers' representatives, sales agents or brokers. In most cases, however, the sales force plays a major role. In companies that sell business products, such as ABB or Du Pont, the salespeople may be the only contact. To these customers, the sales force is the company. In consumer product companies, such as Nike or Unilever, that sell through intermediaries, final consumers rarely meet salespeople or even know about them. Still, the sales force plays an important behind-the-scenes role. It works with wholesalers and retailers to gain their support and to help them to be more effective in selling the company's products.

Advantages of Personal Selling

One key advantage personal selling has over other promotional methods is that it is a two-way form of communication. In selling situations the message sender (e.g. a salesperson) can adjust the message as they gain feedback from message receivers (e.g. a customer). So if a customer does not understand the initial message (e.g. doesn't fully understand how the product works) the salesperson can make adjustments to address questions or concerns. Many non-personal forms of promotion, such as a radio advertisement, are inflexible, at least in the short-term, and cannot be easily adjusted to address audience questions.

The interactive nature of personal selling also makes it the most effective promotional method for building relationships with customers, particularly in the business-to-business market. This is especially important for companies that either sell expensive products or sell lower cost but high volume products (i.e., buyers must purchase in large quantities) that rely heavily on customers making repeat purchases. Because such purchases may take a considerable amount of time to complete and may involve the input of many people at the purchasing company (i.e., the buying center), sales success often requires the marketer develop and maintain strong relationships with members of the purchasing company.

Finally, personal selling is the most practical promotional option for reaching customers who are not easily reached through other methods. The best example is in selling to the business market where, compared to the consumer market, advertising, public relations and sales promotions are often not well received.

Main Disadvantages of Personal Selling

The main disadvantage of personal selling is the cost of employing a sales force. Sales people are expensive. In addition to the basic pay package, a business needs to provide incentives to achieve sales (typically this is based on commission and/or bonus arrangements) and the equipment to make sales calls (car, travel and subsistence costs, mobile phone etc). In addition, a sales person can only call on one customer at a time. This is not a cost-effective way of reaching a large audience.

(Adapted from Paul Christ, *Know This: Marketing Basics,* 2nd Edition, KnowThis Media, 2012)

 Reading 2

What Makes A Good Salesperson?

When you say a person is a born salesperson, what do you consider to be the attributes a person might possess that would lead you to draw that conclusion?

Invariably the characteristics always seem to be that he or she is a good talker, has the "gift of gab", an outgoing personality, is charming, friendly, has a sense of humor, is engaging, quite persuasive and has personality plus.

While these traits are seen frequently in those who sell, would you consider them characteristics of a true sales professional?

While they could be, I have found that there are other characteristics that are far more important.

A charming, outgoing personality can be very magnetic but, as with any relationship, the luster can fade if there is nothing substantial behind it.

I find that people are looking for a salesperson who is honest, has integrity, is truthful, and, most importantly, cares about the needs of his or her clients and possesses a genuine desire to serve them.

In-depth research of the top three percent of outstanding sales professionals throughout the country has shown that these top performers share two common characteristics—the ability to establish rapport with their customers and the consistent creation of an atmosphere of trust in all their sales relationships.

I find many times sales executives are confused by, or even unaware of, the difference between customers simply buying a product or service and a salesperson actually selling.

Just because a customer has parted with his or her money in exchange for a product or service does not mean that a sale has occurred.

For example, a prospect walks into a retail establishment to buy a blouse and the salesperson successfully finds the type of blouse, determines the occasion for which it is intended and how it will fit in with the prospect's current wardrobe. Then she writes up the order. Despite the fact that this may seem to be an act of selling on the salesperson's part, it really isn't. This scenario is merely an example of a salesperson filling a customer's order.

By contrast, the salesperson, in addition to selecting the correct blouse for her customer, may ask a few questions about the customer's current wardrobe needs and learns that her client has just landed a new job.

This reveals that the customer's real need is for professional clothing that will make a positive impression in her new workplace. The salesperson then proceeds to show the customer a new line of high-end designer suits and coordinating accessories the store has recently received—and the customer walks out with not only the intended blouse but also a suit, matching shoes, a handbag and scarf.

This is the act of selling. It is not just filling an order but, instead, establishing rapport, gaining trust, determining a need and then meeting that need.

(Roy Chitwood, "What are the traits of very good sales people" from http://www.maxsacks.com/articles/article0106.html)

About the Author

Roy Chitwood is an author, trainer and consultant in sales and sales management and is the president of Max Sacks International, Seattle.

Question

Can you share with your classmates an example of a good salesperson?

 Activity 1

What Are the Steps in the Selling Process?

Check the following words in your dictionary, and put the right word in the right blank below. You have to know that one word usually has different meanings. You have to decide the right meaning of a word according to the context it is used in.

> preapproach; presentation; approach; prospecting ; closing; follow-up; handling objections

Most training programs view the selling process as consisting of several steps that the salesperson must master. These steps focus on the goal of getting new customers and obtaining orders from them.

The first step in the selling process is _____, which means identifying qualified potential customers. Approaching the right potential customers is crucial to selling success. The salesperson must often approach many prospects to get just a few sales. Although the company supplies some leads, salespeople need skill in finding their own.

Before calling on a prospect, the salesperson should learn as much as possible about the organization (what it needs, who is involved in the buying) and its buyers (their characteristics and buying styles). This step is known as the _____. The salesperson can consult standard industry and online sources, acquaintances, and others to learn about the company. Another task is to decide on the best approach, which might be a personal visit, a phone call, or a letter.

During the _____ step, the salesperson should know how to meet and greet the buyer and get the relationship off to a good start. This step involves the salesperson's appearance, opening lines, and the follow-up remarks. The opening lines should be positive and followed by some key questions to learn more about the customer's needs or by showing a display or sample to attract the buyer's attention and curiosity.

During the _____ step of the selling process, the salesperson tells the product "story" to the buyer, showing how the product will make or save money. The salesperson describes the product features but concentrating on presenting customer benefits.

Customers almost always have objections during the presentation or when asked to place an order. The problem can be either logical or psychological, and objections are often unspoken. In _____, the salesperson should use positive approach, seek out hidden objections, ask the buyer to clarify any objections, take objections as opportunities to provide more information, and turn the objections into reasons for buying.

After handling the prospect's objections, the salesperson now tries to close the sale. Some salespeople do not get around to _____ or do not handle it well. They may lack confidence, feel guilty about asking for the order, or fail to recognize the right moment to close the sale. Salespeople can use one of several closing techniques. They can ask for the order, review points of agreement, offer to help write up the order, ask whether the buyer wants this model or that one, or note that the buyer will lose out if the order is not placed now. The salesperson may offer the buyer special reasons to close, such as lower price or an extra quantity at no charge.

The last step in the selling process is _____, which is necessary if the salesperson wants to ensure customer satisfaction and repeat business. The salesperson should schedule a call when the initial order is received to make sure there is proper installation, instruction and servicing. This can increase customer satisfaction and might lead to repeat buying.

Application

Your life tomorrow is created by the choices you make today. Today, choose to be your own boss. Live the life you deserve — start over, start fresh, start now.

Suppose that you have decided to be an Avon (雅芳) Representative, which means you will sell Avon cosmetics directly to the consumers. To learn more about Avon's direct selling program, please visit www.avon.com.

Regarding to the above mentioned selling steps, work in groups, and design a plan of selling Avon cosmetics to a customer. Then share the plan of your group with other groups in your class.

Activity 2

How to Talk to Your Customer

The deeper the dialogue, the greater the sales results.

—Linda Richardson

Suggestion 1: Open with a focus on your customer.

Task: David is a sales representative of a photocopier manufacturer. He was introduced by a friend John to meet Bill, an office manager. Compare the following two openings, which is more effective? Why?

Opening 1: "Bill, John said you might be interested in the new things we are doing in research with photocopying, so I'm here to talk with you about our newly developed photocopier."

Opening 2: "Bill, thanks for taking the time to meet with me. I know how busy you are and I appreciate the time. John said you are doing some interesting things in improving work efficiency. I've given thought to that and looked at your new web site, which looks great. I'd like to learn more about what you are doing and see whether I can be of some help. How does that sound?"

Suggestion 2: Develop a dialogue to determine deeper needs. When a customer tells you something, don't immediately respond with an answer. Instead of being the answer man or answer woman, acknowledge the comment and, when appropriate, find out more by asking a "Why" question. Take a moment to show your thoughtful consideration.

Task: Consider this simple situation. The customer asks, "Does this shirt come in a more neutral color?" Below are some responses that salespeople might use. Discuss with your group members, which are better? Why?

A: — "Yes. It comes in a light brown color."

B: — "No. Only one color. But it's the latest color."

C: — "Oh, so what you are saying is you don't like the color? If I can get it light brown, then will you buy it?"

D: — "Well, the quality is excellent. The fabric is soft and comfortable."

E: — "Oh, is the color too bright? Most customers feel it is very neutral."

F: — "Oh, we offer a variety of choices. May I ask which color you prefer?"

G: — "You look so elegant and don't want to be too shiny, right? Are you going to wear it in the office or outdoors?"

H: — "I agree that a more neutral color might suit you better. If you don't mind, may I know what kind of job you are doing?"

Suggestion 3: When handling objections, use acknowledgment (I understand) and empathy (I care).

Task: When you are presenting your new product to your customers, one of the customers complains: "Your people are always spouting formulas as if we know what to do with them!" Which of the following is a better response? Why?

A: "What is it you don't understand? I'll go over the process again."

B: "We certainly don't mean to do that. I'm sorry we have not been clear. What specific part should we explain again?"

Suggestion 4: Appropriate praise is key to approaching your customer.

Task: Read the following two dialogues. Which salesperson, Rep A or B, can get the order? Why?

Dialogue One

Rep A: "Is anybody here? I'm from the Danlin Company. Sorry to disturb you. May I ask some questions about your cash register?"

Boss A: "Do you mean that something is wrong with our cash register?"

Rep A: "I don't mean that. I'm just thinking that you might want to change to a new one."

Boss A: "My cash register works quite well and looks like a new one. I'm not considering changing to a new one."

Rep A: "It does not work as well as you think. The store next to you has changed to a new cash register."

Boss A: "Thank you for coming. I'll contact you later."

Dialogue Two

Rep B: "Is Mr. Zheng here? I'm from the Dahua Company. Sorry for disturbing you. I am in charge of the local sales of our company. Whenever I pass by your shop, I always see lots of customers in your shop. You must run a very good business."

Boss B: "Thank you. Actually the business is not as good as it looks."

Rep B: "I observe that the shop assistants treat the customers quite well. You must have given them lots of training. Because of my work, I often go to shops. I've found that few do as well as yours. Mr. Wu, the boss of the store next door, appreciates your management too."

Boss B: "Mr. Wu? Does he? Actually he's doing quite well."

Rep B: "You are right. Mr. Wu just bought a new cash register from me yesterday and he mentioned that you might need one too. That's why I'm here today."

Boss B: "Oh, he changed to a new one!"

Rep B: "A new one can increase the current speed by 30%. Your customers will not need to wait so long, and you can service more customers. Will Mr. Zheng consider buying a new one?"

 Activity 3

Translation and Discussion (13)

Translate the following story and the questions into English, and then discuss the questions in English.

顾客到服装店买衣服，一般都要试穿，满意后才会购买。在这个过程中，店面销售员的体态、语言都会对顾客的购买决策产生很多的影响。正是因为这样，服装店在店员的选择上很慎重，并很注重对店员的培训。

问题
1. 你认为在招聘店员时要考虑哪些方面的条件？
2. 服装店可以采取哪些方法来激励店员？

 Supplementary Material

Six Critical Skills of Making Sales Talk

Top performers often say that their sales dialogues feel more like brainstorming with their customers than "selling". These are the six critical skills that are fundamental to making their dialogues so fluid and productive.

Presence — communicating energy, conviction, and interest when speaking and listening;

Relating — building rapport, using acknowledgment, and expressing empathy to connect with customers;

Questioning — creating a logical questioning strategy and effectively using probing skills to uncover needs;

Listening — understanding what the customer communicates in words, tone, and body language;

Positioning — persuasively demonstrating value and application to the customer by customizing your product knowledge to the needs of the customer;

Checking — eliciting feedback on what you have said to gauge customer understanding and agreement.

These skills are the tools of selling. The sharper the skills, the more effective the salesperson. A weakness in any one of the skills puts a cap on effectiveness. For example, if the salesperson can't establish rapport with the customer, it is unlikely the customer will open up in answering questions. If the salesperson is a poor listener, answers lose their value. And without an understanding of customer needs, it's almost impossible to connect capabilities to customer needs.

Dialogue selling requires product knowledge and technical expertise, but equal to these is customer knowledge and skill. In dialogue selling, the salesperson becomes a resource person who, because he or she fully understands that particular customer's specific needs, can meet the needs that relate to his or her product and also cross-sell and meet the customer's broader spectrum of needs. To succeed in dialogue selling, you must master the six critical skills.

(Adapted from Linda Richardson, The Sales Success Handbook: 20 Lessons to Open and Close Sales Now, McGraw-Hill, 2006.)

Application

1. You've got a part-time job as a salesperson selling cell phones. Create a dialogue with a customer (who can be played by one of your classmates). Demonstrate the six skills when talking to the customer.

2. Besides the six skills, do you have any other suggestions to the salespeople?

Unit 14

On-line Marketing

After learning this unit, you will be able to answer the following questions.

- What arethe challenges of on-line marketing?
- What is E-commerce?
- What are the methods of on-line marketing?
- On-line Marketing
- Who are on-line consumers?
- What are the benefits of on-line marketing?

 Warm-up

  Technology used in online marketing has advanced to a state where collection, enhancement and aggregation of information are instantaneous. Have you ever clicked any advertisement on the Internet? What do you think of the ads springing up when you are surfing online?

Reading 1

What is E-commerce?

Electronic commerce is a term for any type of business or commercial transaction which involves the transfer of information across the Internet. It covers a range of different types of businesses, from consumer based retail sites, through auction or music sites, to business exchanges trading goods and services between corporations. It is currently one of the most important aspects of the Internet.

E-commerce allows consumers to electronically exchange goods and services with no barriers of time or distance. Electronic commerce has expanded rapidly over the past five years and is predicted to continue at this rate, or even accelerate. In the near future the boundaries between "conventional" and "electronic" commerce will become increasingly blurred as more and more businesses move sections of their operations onto the Internet.

Business to Business or B2B refers to commerce between businesses rather than between a business and a consumer. B2B businesses often deal with hundreds or even thousands of other businesses, either as customers or suppliers. Carrying out these transactions electronically provides vast competitive advantages over traditional methods. When implemented properly, e-commerce is often faster, cheaper and more convenient than the traditional methods of bartering goods and services.

The road to creating a successful online store can be difficult if you are unaware of e-commerce principles and what e-commerce is supposed to do for your online business. Researching and understanding the guidelines required to properly implement an e-business plan is a crucial part to become successful with online store building.

To better understand what e-commerce is all about, you may think about something happening in your life. Do you want to buy a gift for someone or send a greeting card or a box of chocolate? Do you want to buy a concert ticket or better yet, an airline ticket to London, reserve a hotel room, or do business with your suppliers? Then you can go online. It's that simple! It's all about doing business online—the e-commerce way. E-commerce is not about just online stores, it's about anything and everything to do with money. If you start to pay online, e-commerce is about to make an introduction into your life soon.

Exercises

I. Concept Check

1. E-commerce is a _____ for any type of _____, or _____, which involves the transfer of information across the Internet.

2. _____ or B2B refers to _____ between _____ rather than

between a business and a consumer.

II. Discussion

1. Have you ever bought something online? If yes, what have you bought? If no, why?

2. What do you know about those famous web sites such as Taobao.com, Jingdong.com, and Dangdang.com? Have you ever had any experience involving these web sites?

3. What, in your opinion, can people benefit from e-commerce?

4. Do you think e-commerce will bring some risks? What are the potential risks?

5. Do you think e-commerce will replace completely the actual business activities happening off-line?

Have a group discussion about "Who are on-line consumers?" Write down your answer in the following table.

Who Are Online Consumers

Customers	The goods they may purchase
1.	
2.	
3.	
4.	
5.	

Reading 2

What Are the Benefits of On-line Marketing ?

Online marketing has only recently made its foray, and yet its charm, speed and time saving attributes have made it a viable option. Sitting on your chair and just a mouse clicking away to make a purchase, seems so simple and effortless that eyebrows are raised. Internet marketing has become an energetic and economical way to buy products and services in less time and with less energy.

E-commerce also allows for higher profit margins, since your costs are low, you make more profit from sales. Marketing is an integral part of sales; offline advertisements costs can burn a hole in your pocket, whereas online you can submit free ads, do ad swaps with **e-zines** or use pay per click search engines, etc.

Online advertising offers a unique combination of scalability, cost-effectiveness, desirable **demographics**, highly targeted marketing, a rapidly growing audience and unmatched tracking capabilities. Here are more details about these benefits and other things Web advertising can offer:

The first thing comes with scalability. Like television **commercials**, it doesn't cost very much to increase the reach of an online ad campaign. There's no need to print additional copies of a magazine or to create and send direct mail pieces. Expanding the size of your ad campaign can be as easy as sending an email or clicking on a Web page.

On-line ads bring about hot demographics. The online community is more affluent, better educated, younger and more willing to spend money than the population at large—even as more and more people go online.

Targeted messages are available. Unlike broadcast and print media, the Internet allows advertisers to target exactly who will see their ads and in what context. Web publications serve every conceivable audience, from the mass market to obscure niche groups, making it easier for advertisers to find a receptive market for their products and services.

The Internet also ensures broad and flexible reach. Although the Internet can't yet match television's market penetration, the size of the online audience is growing very quickly. More importantly, because you promote online ads by the impression, you can buy as much or as little of that audience as you desire.

On-line ads offer deep content. Unlike commercials or print ads, many web ads offer the tools to help create a right landing page, full of unique content. While the listing page is the only beginning to exposing contents on the web, potential customers can always click to go directly to the desired Web site. Once there, they can access as much material about the company and products as they would like.

On-line ads come along with detailed tracking and measurement. Compared to online advertising, traditional media advertising is like shooting in the dark. Many Web sites allow advertisers to gather detailed information on who saw an ad, when, in what context, how many times the ad was clicked and so on. Better yet, the ad launcher gets this information instantly, allowing them to adjust their ad campaign and make it even more effective.

On-line ads have great ability to extend the transaction. Traditionally, advertising was a one-way mechanism. Apart from techniques like **toll-free** numbers pitched in infomercials and mail-in **coupons** inserted into print publications, there was no way for customers to act on the information in the ad. On the Web, though, interested customers can click, learn more and actually buy on the spot. There's simply nothing more powerful.

New online ad technologies flourish quickly. The old-fashioned, static banner ad is giving way to a new generation of ads that use animation, video and even **built-in** e-commerce capabilities. These ads can deliver more information to customers and make it easier for them to learn about the company's products.

Notes

① E-zine: *n.* electronic magazine 电子杂志

② commercial: *n.* a commercially sponsored ad on radio or television 商业广告

③ demographics: *n.* a statistic characterizing human populations (or segments of human populations broken down by age or sex or income etc.) (尤指市场测算的) 人口统计数据

④ toll-free: *adj.* having no toll levied for its use 免费的

⑤ coupon: *n.* a negotiable certificate that can be detached and redeemed as needed 订单、优惠券、配给券

⑥ built-in: *adj.* existing as an essential constituent or characteristic 嵌入的，内装的

Exercises

Fill-in the blanks.

1. On-line advertising offers a unique combination of_____, _____, _____, _____, _____, a rapidly growing _____ and unmatched _____.

2. Web publications serve _____, from the _____ to obscure _____, making it easier for _____ to find a _____ for their products and services.

3. Unlike _____ or _____, many on-line ads offer the tools to help create a _____, full of _____.

4. Partly because you pay only for exactly what you're getting, on-line advertising can be extremely _____ with other forms of advertising.

5. Traditionally, advertising was a _____.

6. The old-fashioned, static banner ad is giving way to a new generation of ads that use _____, _____ and even _____.

 **Activity 1**

Methods of On-line Marketing

Online advertising is a form of promotion that uses the Internet and World Wide Web for the expressed purpose of delivering marketing messages to attract customers. The followings are some major methods of online marketing.

Online video directories for brands are a good example of interactive advertising. These directories complement television advertising and allow the viewer to view the commercials of a number of brands. If the advertiser has opted for a response feature, the viewer may then choose to visit the brand's website, or interact with the advertiser through other touch points such as email, chat or phone.

Floating ad: An ad which moves across the user's screen or floats above the content.

Trick banner: A banner ad that looks like a dialog box with buttons. It simulates an error message or an alert.

Pop-up: A new window which opens in front of the current one, displaying an advertisement, or entire webpage.

Pop-under: Similar to a Pop-Up except that the window is loaded or sent behind the current window so that the user does not see it until they close one or more active windows.

Video ad: Similar to a banner ad, except that instead of a static or animated image, actual moving video clips are displayed.

Ⅰ. *Discuss the merits and demerits of the on-line marketing methods mentioned above, and try to finish the following statements.*

You are selling costumes designed by yourself. The best way to market your costumes on-line is _____, because _____.

You are a cosmetics salesperson for a big company. The best way to market your products on-line is _____, because _____.

You are a bookseller. You can market the books by _____, because _____.

Your company specializes in digital camera sales. You can market your products on-line by _____, because _____.

Your company is a trading company mainly dealing with Chinese handicrafts. You can market on-line by _____, because _____.

Ⅱ. *Search the Internet and determine the main features of the following websites.*

Website	Features
www.elong.com	
www.zhaopin.com	
shop.vipshop.com	
www.taobao.com	
www.youku.com	

 Activity 2

The Following Is the Ad of WorldPay Corp.

For millions of people around the world, WorldPay is the way to pay—trusted and secure.

An important part of The Royal Bank of Scotland Group, the 5th biggest banking group in the world, WorldPay payment solutions are trusted by thousands of businesses, big and small.

Our customers accept payments over the Internet, by phone, fax and mail. They accept Visa, MasterCard, Diners, American Express, JCB and all the major credit cards. Not forgetting debit cards and local payment schemes like Maestro, Laser, Electron and more. Bank transfers (such as the German ELV system), installments, standing-order and direct-debit style payments. All in their customer's currency and language—wherever they are in the world.

WorldPay is the only way to accept such a universal range of payments through one merchant account, one payment processing system.

Elemental and easy too. The way to accept a world of payments.

Application

Discuss online payment in mainland China. How many payment methods do you know and have you ever tried one of them? What are their merits and demerits? Complete the following table.

Methods	Merits	Demerits

 Activity 3

Translation and Discussion (14)

Translate the following story and the questions into English, and then discuss the questions in English.

现在网上购物的人越来越多了。网上购物一是可以不受时间地点的限制，二是价格比实体店便宜。但是网上商店不能提供试穿服务，也不能看到实物。经过调查，开朗他们了解到，现在的职业女性大多是网民，喜欢在网上购物的也不少。所以他们考虑是否也在网上开个店。

问题

1. 你认为他们有必要在网上开店吗？

2. 你所认识的中年职业女性有人在网上购买衣服吗？跟她们聊一聊，了解她们主要购买哪种类型的衣服；对于不在网上购买衣服的人，也请了解她们不购买的理由。

Supplementary Material

What Are the Challenges of On-line Marketing?

Internet marketing requires customers to use newer technologies rather than traditional media. Low-speed Internet connections are another barrier. If companies build large or overly-complicated websites, individuals connected to the Internet via dial-up connections or mobile devices may experience significant delays in content delivery.

From the buyer's perspective, the inability of shoppers to touch, smell, taste or "try on" tangible goods before making an online purchase can be limiting. However, there is an industry standard for e-commerce vendors to reassure customers by having liberal return policies as well as providing in-store pick-up services.

A survey of 410 marketing executives listed the following barriers to entry for large companies looking to market on-line: insufficient ability to measure impact, lack of internal capability, and difficulty of convincing senior management.

Information security is important both to companies and consumers that participate in on-line business. Many consumers are hesitant to purchase items over the Internet because they do not trust that their personal information will remain private. Encryption is the primary method for implementing privacy policies. Recently some companies that do business on-line have been caught leaking customers' information by giving away or selling the information to other companies. Several of these companies provide guarantees on their websites, claiming that customer information will remain private. Some companies that purchase customer information offer the option for individuals to have their information removed from the database, also known as opting out. However, many customers are unaware if and when their information is being shared, and are unable to stop the transfer of their information between companies if such activity occurs.

Another major security concern is whether consumers that trade with e-commerce merchants will receive exactly what they purchase. On-line merchants have attempted to address this concern by investing in and building strong consumer brands (e.g., Amazon.com, eBay, Overstock.com), and by leveraging merchant/feedback rating systems and e-commerce bonding solutions. All of these solutions attempt to assure consumers that their transactions will be free of problems because the merchants can be trusted to provide reliable products and services. Additionally, the major on-line payment mechanisms (credit cards, PayPal, Google Checkout, etc.) have also provided back-end (后台的) buyer protection systems to address problems if they actually do occur.

Questions

1 Have you ever experienced any problems in on-line buying? What were they?
2 In your opinion, what are the ways to improve safety of e-commerce?

Supplementary Vocabulary

authentication	身份认证
mobile bank	手机银行
bar coding	条形码
password	密码
credit cards	信用卡
refund	退款
order	下单
logistics	物流
express	快递
parcel	包裹
shopping cart	购物车
online payment	网上支付
disbursement services	支付服务
double spending	重复付款
e-wallet	电子钱包
electronic funds transfer (EFT)	电子资金转账
e-cash	电子现金
e-catalogs	电子商品目录
e-checks	电子支票
Alipay	支付宝
Network shield	网盾

Unit 15

International Marketing

After learning this unit, you will be able to answer the following questions.

- How can one adapt to the environment of international marketing?
- What is international marketing?
- **International Marketing**
- How can one enter the international market?
- What factors need to be considered when going international?

Warm-up

Have you found any store that sells clothes originally made for the foreign market? If the clothes are made for export, why are they sold in the domestic market? Would you buy clothes from these stores? Why or why not?

(Picture from http://image.baidu.com/)

 Reading 1

What is International Marketing?

Today we might be seeing the triumph of international marketing. Governments all over the world are encouraging market-based activities. In past centuries, international trade was conducted and had broad and simultaneous impact on nations, firms and individuals. As a result, many countries and firms have found it highly desirable to become major participants in international marketing. Many managers have to face the increasing globalization of markets and competition. Even the biggest companies in the biggest home markets cannot survive on domestic sales alone, if they are in global industries such as cars, banking, consumer electronics, entertainment, pharmaceuticals, publishing, travel services, or home appliances.

International marketing is the process of planning and conducting transactions across national borders to create exchanges that satisfy the objectives of individuals and organizations. International marketing of a firm may go through several stages of international involvement. In the first stage, the firm's root and development are mainly in the domestic market, it has no current ambitions of expanding abroad, and does not perceive any significant competitive threat from abroad. Such a firm may eventually get some orders from abroad, which are usually regarded as less important compared with domestic sales. When this direct export grows, the overseas market would draw attention and the firm begins to take it more seriously and puts more efforts into exporting.

Direct exporting brings great profits, and the firm may come to the second stage—entering the overseas market itself, establishing its own distribution or marketing network in the targeted market. However, in the beginning when entering the overseas market, the firm can tend to treat each overseas market individually and neglect the similarities which may exist between the countries entered. This can result in an overlapping overseas organization and a tremendous cost increase.

The third stage is closely related to the expansion of overseas markets. In order to optimize management and facilitate international trade, the firm tends to analyze the overseas markets and tries to apply efficient marketing strategies. Research may be conducted to determine the similarities and differences of overseas markets. The classification of overseas markets will be helpful for the marketers to decide how to reduce costs and increase efficiency across borders. The targeted markets would be treated in groups. Similar markets would be put under similar marketing management systems, and the marketing team is able to allocate the available resources reasonably.

Finally, the firm may develop a global marketing strategy as the international trade rockets. In the global stage, the focus centers on the entire World market. All decisions will be made to optimize the product's position across markets—of course the home country is no longer the center of the product.

Firms have benefited substantially from global marketing expansion. With wider market reached and more customers, firms in the international market produce more efficiently than their domestic-only counterparts do. Firms also learn from their competitors, and can recruit and develop the best talents from all over the world. They grow more than twice as fast in sales and earn significantly higher returns on equity and assets.

Consumers are the greatest beneficiaries of all. They are offered an unprecedented degree of product availability and choice. Furthermore, due to international competition, these products usually offer low prices and better quality. For the first time in history, international goods and service availability have gone beyond the reach of the elite and have become a reasonable expectation for the majority of the population.

Yet, in spite of all these achievements, international marketing faces challenges. Many practitioners refuse to participate in the global market—judging either the market to be too dangerous or themselves too unprepared.

(Adapted from Michael R. Czinkota & Ilkka A. Ronkainen, *International Marketing*, South-Western Cengage Learning, 2010, Chapter 1)

Exercises

Application

Use the Internet to research information about Lenovo, the biggest computer manufacturer in China. Determine its stages of going international. Share the information with your classmates.

First stage _____

Second stage _____

Third stage _____

More _____

Group Discussion

Discuss with your partner about the following questions.

1. Can you name some companies that operate internationally?

2. What benefits will the international marketing bring to Chinese local companies?

3. What risks will a company face in international marketing?

4. Can ordinary consumers benefit from the international marketing of companies?

5. In the city where you live, are there any promising local enterprises which you think should go international? Can you make some suggestions for their international marketing?

 Reading 2

Deciding Whether to Go International

Not all companies need to venture into international markets to survive. For example, many companies are local businesses that need to market well only in the local marketplace. Operating domestically is easier and safer. Managers need not learn another country's language and laws, deal with volatile currencies, face political and legal uncertainties, or redesign their products to suit different customer needs and expectations. However, companies that operate in global industries, where there strategic positions in specific markets are affected strongly by their overall global positions, must compete on a worldwide basis if they are to succeed.

Any of several factors might draw a company into the international arena. Global competitors might attack the company's domestic market by offering better products or lower prices. The company might want to counterattack these competitors in their home markets to tie up their resources. Or the company might discover foreign markets that present higher profit opportunities than the domestic market does. The company's domestic market might be stagnant or shrinking, or the company might need an enlarged customer base in order to achieve economies of scale. The company might want to reduce its dependence on any one market so as to reduce its risk. Finally, the company's customers might be expanding abroad and require international servicing.

Before going abroad, the company must weigh several risks and answer many questions about its ability to operate globally. Can the company learn to understand the preferences and buying behavior of consumers in other countries? Can it offer competitively attractive products? Will it be able to adapt to other countries' business cultures and deal effectively with foreign nationals? Do the company's mangers have the necessary international experience? Has management considered the impact of regulations and the political environments of other countries?

Because of the risks and difficulties of entering international markets, most companies do not act until some situation or event thrusts them into the global arena. Someone—a domestic exporter, a foreign importer, a foreign government—may ask the company to sell abroad. Or the company may be saddled with overcapacity and must find additional markets for its goods.

Before going abroad, the company should try to define its international marketing objectives and policies. It should decide what volume of foreign sales it wants. Most companies start small when they go abroad. Some plan to stay small, seeing international sales as a small part of their business. Other companies have bigger plans, seeing international business as equal to or even more important than their domestic business.

The company must also choose how many countries it wants to market in. Generally, it makes sense to operate in fewer countries with deeper commitment and penetration in each. The **Bulova Watch Company** decided to operate in many international markets and expanded into more than 100 countries. As a result, it spread itself too thin, made profit in only two countries, and lost around $40 million. In contrast, although consumer product company **Amway** is now breaking into markets at a furious pace, it is doing so only after decades of gradually building up its overseas presence. Known for its neighbor-to-neighbor direct-selling networks, Amway expanded into Australia in 1971, a country far away but similar to the U.S. market. Then, in the 1980s, Amway expanded into 10 more countries, and the pace increased rapidly from then on. By 1994, Amway was firmly established in 60 countries. Entering the new millennium, international proceeds account for over 70 percent of the company's overall sales.

Next, the company needs to decide on the types of countries to enter. A country's attractiveness depends on the product, geographical factors, income and population, political climate, and other factors.

After listing possible international markets, the company must screen and rank each one. **Colgate**'s decision to enter the Chinese market seems fairly simple and straightforward: China is a huge market without established competition. Given the huge population, the market can grow even larger. Yet we still can question whether market size alone is reason enough for selecting China. Colgate also must consider other factors: Will the Chinese government remain stable and supportive? Does China provide for the production and distribution technologies needed to produce and market Colgate's products profitably? Will Colgate be able to overcome cultural barriers and convince Chinese consumers to brush their teeth regularly? Can Colgate compete effectively with dozens of local competitors? Colgate's current success in China suggests that it could answer yes to all of these questions. Still, the company's future in China is filled with uncertainties.

Possible global markets should be ranked on several factors, including market size, market growth, cost of doing business, competitive advantage, and risk level. The goal is to determine the potential of each market and then decide which markets offer the greatest long-run return on investment.

(Adapted from Philip Kotler & Gary Armstrong, *Principles of Marketing*, 9th edition. Tsinghua University Press, 2001, Chapter 19.)

Notes

Bulova Watch Company: 宝路华手表公司

Amway: 安利公司

Colgate: 高露洁公司

Application

Amway is a US-based health care product manufacturer. It adopts a special business model which offers business opportunities to every individual distributor. Go to the website of this company and any related channel to understand its story. Evaluate the advantages and disadvantages of its first going into the Chinese market.

 Going into the Chinese Market?	
Advantages	**Disadvantages**

Activity 1

How to Enter the International Market?

For most companies, the most significant international marketing decision they are likely to take is how they could enter new markets. However, there is no ideal market entry strategy. The decision is made to a large extent by the firm's objectives and attitudes to international marketing. Besides direct exporting, there are many other market entry strategies available.

Agents: Agents are independent individuals or firms who are contracted to act on behalf of exporters to obtain orders on a commission basis. They typically represent a number of manufacturers and will handle a number of non-competitive items.

Distributors: They buy the products from the manufacturer and seek the exclusive rights for a specific sales territory and generally represent the manufacturer in all aspects of sales and service in that area.

Franchising: Franchising is a simple way for a manufacturer to enter an international market. The company enters into an agreement with a licensee in the foreign market. For a fee or royalty, the licensee buys the right to use the company's manufacturing process, trademark, patent, trade secret, or other items of value. The company thus gains entry into the market at little risk; the licensee gains production expertise or a well known product or name without having to start from scratch.

Wholly-owned subsidiaries: For any firm, the most expensive method of market entry is likely to be the development of its own foreign subsidiary. It requires the greatest investment of management time and commitment. It can only be undertaken when demand for the market appears to be assured, and the firm is taking a long-term view.

Company acquisition: For many Western companies, particularly those from the UK and USA, the pressure to produce short-term profits means that speed of market entry is essential and this can be achieved by acquiring an existing company in the market, which gives immediate access to a trained labor force, existing customer and supplier contacts, recognized brands, an established distribution network and an immediate source of revenue.

Joint venture: It means joining with foreign companies to produce or market products or services. This is usually based on the premise that two or more companies can provide complementary competitive advantages for the new company to exploit.

(Adapted from Isobel Doole and Robin Lowe, *International Marketing Strategy: Analysis, Development and Implementation,* Cengage Learning, 2012)

Case study

Volvo Cars now officially owned by Chinese Geely!

When Zhejiang Geely Holding Group Company Limited (Geely) completed its acquisition of the Volvo Car Corporation from Ford Motor Company in 2010, it shocked the world immediately. Geely was established in 1986 and launched its auto manufacturing business in 1997. With only 13 years of experience in car manufacturing, Geely has acquired Volvo which has existed for more than 80 years and is well-known globally.

It is true that most Chinese automobile companies entered the international market later than their foreign counterparts, so Chinese cars have lower brand recognition overseas. The acquisition of Volvo has greatly boosted Geely's brand value and brand recognition overseas. It has also helped strengthen the confidence of overseas partners to cooperate with Geely.

However, According to Geely's Chairman Li Shufu's point of view, Geely is Geely and Volvo is Volvo. Geely is a popular brand and Volvo is more of a luxury brand. He does not place too much hope of Geely's future on Volvo. "Cross-border acquisition is not the only way for a domestic brand to achieve global development. Our lifeline depends on realizing scientific and technological innovation, " Li Shufu said.

Discussion

1. Besides Geely, do you know any other Chinese company that acquired a foreign company?

2. What are the benefits as well as challenges to Geely by acquiring Volvo?

 **Activity 2**

How to Adapt to the Foreign Marketing Environment?

Since KFC opened the first outlet in Beijing in 1987, the fast-food giant has occupied its dominant position in China. As KFC expands rapidly in China, it formulates specific strategy aiming to Chinese customers and accomplishes unprecedented success. The prominent success of KFC in China's market can be attributed to its franchise policy and scientific managerial operations, well known as CHAMPS, which measures operational basics like Cleanliness, Hospitality, Accuracy, Maintenance, Product Quality and Speed. Moreover, the accomplishments are the reward towards KFC's comprehensive understanding of Chinese culture and its excellent localization strategies specifically manipulated to meet the characteristic requirements of the estimated 450 million urban Chinese consumers.

In the initial period of KFC's entry into China market, few of Chinese consumers were really impressed with the food itself. Instead, they were more fascinated with the eating experience: the encounter with friendly employees, quick service, spotless floors climate-controlled and brightly-lit dining areas, and smiling Colonel Sanders standing in front of the main gate. Having experienced the initial surprises brought by a never-seen western lifestyle, Chinese consumers have gradually calmed down and their consumption attitudes towards foreign products are getting more reasonable. They are more concerned with the nutrition and tastes of the fast food.

KFC's product strategies are categorized into two aspects. ① To meet consumers' desire for novelty by introducing western style products like Mexican Chicken Warp and New Orleans Barbeque Wings. This means can satisfy young consumers who are more open and acceptable to the foreign flavors. ② To cater to consumers' taste for traditional Chinese meal by offering Chinese style fast food from time to time, say, Old Beijing Chicken Roll, a wrap modeled after the way Peking duck is served, but with fried chicken inside and accompanied with green onions and hoisin sauce and Sichuan Spicy Chicken which absorbs the spicy flavor of Sichuan dish. Chinese-style breakfast food, like porridge is also served since Oct 27, 2003 on the breakfast menu of all 59 KFC restaurants in Shenzhen. The breakfast choices are a blend of East and West, ranging from Chinese seafood and chicken congee, Hong Kong milk tea to Western burgers, potato sticks and orange juice. This measure can attract older consumers who are fond of Chinese food and in need of the convenience of fast food service as well. Based on its scrutiny and adoption of Chinese traditional culinary arts, KFC has developed a series of products which are specially designed for the tastes of Chinese consumers. Moreover, in purpose of maintaining its image of a U.S. brand and keeping consistent with its globalization strategy, most of KFC's Chinese side dishes are defined as short-term products and would be replaced by new products.

To represent the Chinese characteristics and increase the identification from Chinese consumers, KFC absorbs Chinese cultural elements into the arrangements and decorations of its outlets all over China. In 2003, KFC spent 7.6 million RMB (equal to 900,000 US dollars) to redecorate the flagship outlet in Beijing, which is also the world's largest KFC outlet, with the Great Wall, shadowgraph, Chinese kites and other traditional Chinese symbols. In the Chinese New Year of 2003, all the statues of Colonel Sanders in KFC outlets in China were put on the Chinese traditional suits which are known as "Tang suits".

One feature noticeable in KFC's commercials is its preference on the representation of an ancient art form of China—Beijing Opera. It is interesting to find a U.S. fast food brand presents a declining traditional art and attaches pop culture elements with it. One of the commercials depicts a Beijing Opera actor in costume and with make-ups still on his face is about to have his KFC meal. The second commercial exhibits the contradiction and later harmony of a father and son; the roles of father and son stand for two generations and serve as the distinct incarnations for traditional and pop cultures. The screen is divided into two parts: the father is singing Beijing Opera in the left room while the son is dancing with Hip hop music in the right room. They finally get to harmony by eating the Old Beijing Chicken Roll served by the mother. The third commercial starts with a background music which merges the Beijing Opera and electronic midi. The three commercials exemplify KFC's efforts to integrate Chinese traditional culture into the modern pop culture.

(Adapted from Li, D. Do in China as the Chinese Do: An Overview of KFC's Localization Strategies in China. Retrieved 08/2016 from http://lidan.y3k.org/blog/en/2004/04/kfcs-localization-strategies-in-china/)

Group Work

1. By any possible channel, try to figure out how the Chinese value system is different from the U.S. value system.

2. List as many as possible differences between you and your parents regarding value. Work with your classmates, and finish the following chart.

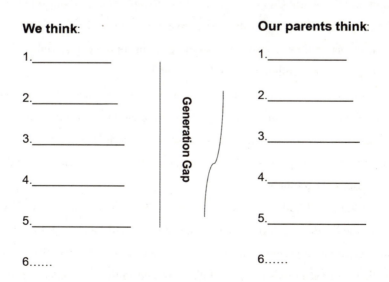

3. Try to find some advertisements of KFC in China. Discuss with your classmates and figure out the reasons that the KFC campaigns won the hearts of Chinese young people.

 Activity 3

Translation and Discussion (15)

Translate the following story and the questions into English, and then discuss the questions in English.

经过几年的打拼,韩柳他们的服装店生意越做越好,越做越大,在好几个城市都开了分店。一天,三个人聚在一起,一边喝咖啡,一边聊着企业的发展规划,寻思着如何才能把企业做大、做强。志成的目标是要把它做成一个国际品牌。

问题
1. 要把服装卖到国际市场有哪些途径?
2. 请你选一个国际服装品牌,上它的网站或通过其他渠道,了解它的国际化历程。把故事与你的同学分享。

 Supplementary Material

Being a Good Sport Globally

In any given country, the majority of corporate sponsorship goes to sports. Of the nearly $25 billion spent worldwide in 2002, two-thirds was allocated to sports. Within sports, the two flagship events are the World Cup in soccer and the Olympic Games (both summer and winter). Sponsors want to align themselves with—and create—meaningful sports-related moments for consumers, at the same time, consumers associate sponsors of sports events with leadership, teamwork, and pursuit of excellence, as well as friendship.

Sponsorships have been a cornerstone of the Coca-Cola Company's marketing efforts for 100 years, having started with using sports stars such as world champion cyclist Bobby Walthour in ads in 1903. Presently, the company is the world's biggest sports sponsor, with total sponsorship-related expenses at $1 billion annually. These activities span different types of sports and various geographies.

Coca-Cola spent $26 million for its sponsorship of the World Cup in 2002, which gave it the right to use the World Cup logo/trademarks, exclusive positioning and branding around the event, as well as premium perimeter advertising positions at every game. Sponsorships include a guarantee that no rival brands can be officially linked to the tournament or use the logo or trademarks to assure exclusivity; FIFA (soccer's governing body) bought all key billboard advertising space around the main stadium for the tournament, and this space was offered to the sponsors first. In addition, every main sponsor got 250 tickets for each game of the tournament for promotional purposes or corporate entertainment (of key constituents, such as intermediaries or customers).

Each country organization within Coca-Cola decides which programs it wants to use during sponsorship depending on its goals, which are jointly set by local managers and headquarters. For example, in Rio de Janeiro, the company erected huge TV screens on which people could watch World Cup games. Given that Ecuador qualified for the tournament for the first time in its history, this fact was played up in local advertising. In Japan, the company used 1-mode phones in addition to traditional media to create meaningful and relevant connections with the World Cup. Naturally, there is always substantial overlap in programs between markets, with headquarters' 20-person team in charge of the coordination effort. One example of this was an online World Cup game that headquarters created in conjunction with Yahoo! and then helped each interested country localize. Another global program was Coca-Cola Go! Stadium Art which allowed consumers and artists to compete to create ads that ran in the various stadiums throughout the tournament. The company also joined forces with other sponsors for cross-promotional efforts, e.g., with Adidas to give away the Official Match Ball, with McDonald's for consumer promotions, and with Toshiba on a cyber cup tournament.

Although marketers have become far more demanding in terms of their sponsorships, the World Cup is one of the few global events available. Pulling out of the World Cup means a competitor stepping in.

While measurement of the return on such investment is challenging, Coca-Cola evaluates such dimensions as the number of new corporate customers that sell Coke in their stores, the incremental amount of promotional/ display activity, and new vending placement. The influence on the brand is the most difficult to establish; World Cup sponsorship has been suggested to have boosted its presence especially in the emerging and developing markets.

Coca-Cola's sports sponsorships

Olympics (since 1928)

● Supports athletes and teams in nearly 200 countries in exchange for exclusive rights in non-alcoholic beverage category through 2008

● Official soft/sports drink (Coca-Cola, PowerAde)

● Runs marketing programs in over 130 countries

Soccer

● FIFA partner since 1974—signed landmark eight-year agreement through 2006 to be official soft/sports drink at Men's World Cup 2002/2006. Women's World Cup 1999/2003, Confederation Cup competitions, under 20/under 17 World Youth Championships

- Also sponsors Copa America, Asian Football Confederation, over 40 national teams
- Basketball
- Signed 100-year agreement in 1998 for Sprite to be official soft drink of NBA/WNBA
- Advertising in over 100 countries

Others
- Coca-Cola Classic: official soft drink of National Football League
- Suge/PowerAde: official sports drink of National Hockey League
- Coca-Cola Classic/Powerade: official soft drink/sports drink of Rugby World Cup
- Sponsor of International Paralympics/Special Olympics

(Adapted from Michael B. Czinkota, Ilkka A. Ronkainen, *International Marketing*, Chapter 18)

Questions

1. Why is Coca-Cola keen on sponsoring sports events and how does it benefit from sponsorship?

2. Do you know any other companies that spend a lot on sponsorship?

Unit 16

Green Marketing

After learning this unit, you will be able to answer the following questions.

- What are the problems of going green?
- What is green marketing?
- Green Marketing
- Why is green marketing important?

Warm-up

Do you like ice cream? Have you ever thought of being in the ice cream business? If you are in the ice cream business, while making, selling and distributing the ice creams, what can you do to protect the environment?

You can go to www.benjerry.com to learn how Ben and Jerry, the co-founders of Ben&Jerry's do in their business.

(Picture from http://image.baidu.com)

Reading 1

What Is Green Marketing?

As society becomes more concerned with the natural environment, businesses have begun to modify their behavior in an attempt to address society's new concern. Some companies have been quick to accept concepts like environment management systems and waste minimization, and have integrated environmental issues into all organizational activities.

One business area where environmental issues have received a great deal of discussion in the popular and professional press is marketing. Terms like "Green Marketing" and "Environmental Marketing" appear frequently in the popular press. Many governments around the world have become so concerned about green marketing activities that they have attempted to regulate them.

Unfortunately, a majority of people believe that green marketing refers solely to the promotion or advertising of products with environmental characteristics. Terms like **Phosphate Free, Recyclable, Refillable, Ozone Friendly and Environmentally Friendly** are some of the things consumers most often associate with green marketing. While these terms are green marketing claims, in general green marketing is a much broader concept, one that can be applied to consumer goods, industrial goods and even services. For example, around the world there are resorts that are beginning to promote themselves as "**ecotourist**" facilities, i.e. facilities that "specialize" in experiencing nature or operating in a fashion that minimizes their environmental impact.

Green Marketing consists of all activities designed to generate and facilitate any exchanges intended to satisfy human needs or wants, such that the satisfaction of these needs and wants occurs, with minimal detrimental impact on natural environment. Thus green marketing incorporates a broad range of activities including product modification, changes to the production process, packaging changes, as well as modifying advertising, etc.

(Adapted from Michael Jay Polonsky: An Introduction to Green Marketing, *Electronic Green Journal*, 1(2), 1994.)

Notes

① phosphate free：无磷的，phosphate-free laundry detergent powder 无磷洗衣粉（含磷污水的排放会造成水域的富营养化。所谓富营养化是指水体中含有大量的磷、氮等植物生长所需的营养物质，造成藻类和其他浮游生物爆发性繁殖，水体中的溶解性氧量下降，水质恶化，导致鱼类和其他生物大量死亡的现象）

② recyclable：可回收的（如废纸可回收利用）

③ refillable：可再装的（如牛奶瓶可收回再使用）

④ ozone friendly：保护臭氧层的（阳光中的强紫外线不仅会引发皮肤癌和加速人的老化，而且对农作物和野生动物也会造成伤害。地球臭氧层是阻挡阳光强紫外线的重要屏障，臭氧层遭到破坏则意味着地球上的生物将受到阳光强紫外线的直接威胁）

⑤ environmentally friendly：保护环境的

⑥ ecotourist：生态旅游者（生态旅游 (ecotourism) 由国际自然保护联盟 (IUCN)1983 年首次提出，1993 年国际生态旅游协会将其定义为：具有保护自然环境和维护当地人民生活双重责任的旅游活动。生态旅游的内涵强调的是对自然景观的保护，强调可持续发展）

Application

The following companies are adopting the green marketing strategy. Can you list more such companies and tell their stories?

Company	Green Marketing Activities
THE BODY SHOP	● Reduce our CO_2 emissions from these activities by 50 per cent, including emissions from electricity, gas and diesel consumption, transporting product from distribution centers to stores, and business travel ● Reduce our electricity consumption for these activities by 50 per cent ● Reduce our waste from these activities by 50 per cent. We want to reduce all the waste created by our stores, offices and distribution centers ● Reduce our domestic water consumption by 25 per cent. Water is an increasingly scarce resource and we want to make sure we don't waste it

Company	Green Marketing Activities
	To reduce CO_2 emissions of "the drink in your hand" by 25%, Coca-Cola will work to reduce the greenhouse gas emissions across its value chain, making comprehensive carbon footprint reductions across its manufacturing processes, packaging formats, delivery fleet, refrigeration equipment and ingredient sourcing
	At a group level, we annually review our management of material issues such as greenhouse gas emissions, water, and sensitive and protected areas. We seek to identify emerging risks and assess methods to reduce them across the company. For example, water scarcity is a potential risk for many of our operations, and we are working to develop tools and processes for our local businesses to use to address this issue
more...	

Reading 2

Why Is Green Marketing Important?

The question of why green marketing has increased importance is quite simple and relies on the basic definition of economics. Economics is the study of how people use their limited resources to try to satisfy unlimited wants.

Mankind has limited resources on earth with which to attempt to provide for the world's unlimited wants. In market societies where there is "freedom of choice", it has been generally accepted that individuals and organizations have the right to attempt to have their wants satisfied. As firms face limited natural resources, they must develop new or alternative ways of satisfying these unlimited wants. Ultimately green marketing looks at how marketing activities utilize these limited resources while satisfying consumers wants, both of individual and industry, as well as achieving the organization objectives.

When looking through the literature there are several suggested reasons for firms' increased use of Green Marketing.

1. Organizations perceive environmental marketing to be an opportunity that can be used to achieve its objectives.

With the more and more serious environmental problem, all types of consumers, both individual and industrial are becoming more concerned and aware about the natural environment. In this situation, firms marketing goods with environmental characteristics will have a competitive advantage over firms marketing non-environmentally responsible alternatives. There are numerous examples of firms who have striven to become more environmentally responsible, in an attempt to better satisfy their consumer needs. For example:

● McDonald's replaced its **clamshell packaging** with waxed paper because of increased consumer concern relating to **polystyrene** production and *ozone depletion*.

● Tuna manufacturers modified their fishing techniques because of the increased concern over **driftnet fishing**, and the resulting death of dolphins.

● Xerox introduced a "high quality" **recycled photocopier paper** in an attempt to satisfy the demands of firms for less environmentally harmful products.

2. Organizations believe they have a moral obligation to be more socially responsible.

Many firms are beginning to realize that they are members of the wider community and therefore must behave in an environmentally responsible fashion. This translates into firms that believe they must achieve environmental objectives as well as profit related objectives. This results in environmental issues being integrated into the firm's corporate culture. Firms in this situation can take two perspectives: ① They can use the fact that they are environmentally responsible as a marketing tool; or ② they can become responsible without promoting this fact.

There are examples of firms adopting both strategies. Organizations like the Body Shop heavily promote the fact that they are environmentally responsible. While this behavior is a competitive advantage, the firm was established specifically to offer consumers environmentally responsible alternatives to conventional cosmetic products. This philosophy is directly tied to the overall corporate culture, rather than simply being a competitive tool.

An example of a firm that does not promote its environmental initiatives is Coca-Cola. They have invested large sums of money in various recycling activities, as well as having modified their packaging to minimize its environmental impact. While being concerned about the environment, Coke has not used this concern as a marketing tool. Thus many consumers may not realize that Coke is a very environmentally committed organization.

3. Governmental bodies are forcing firms to become more responsible.

As with all marketing related activities, governments want to protect consumers and society; this protection has significant Green Marketing implications. Governments establish regulations designed to control the amount of hazardous wastes produced by firms. Many by-products of production are controlled through the issuing of various environmental licenses, thus modifying organizational behavior.

4. Competitors' environmental activities pressure firms to change their environmental marketing activities.

Another major force in the Green Marketing area has been firms' desire to maintain their competitive position. In many cases firms observe competitors promoting their environmental behaviors and attempt to emulate this behavior. In some instances this competitive pressure has caused an entire industry to modify and thus reduce its detrimental environmental behavior. For example, it could be argued that Xerox's "Revive 100% Recycled Paper" was introduced a few years ago in an attempt to address the introduction of recycled photocopier paper by other manufacturers. In another example when one tuna manufacture stopped using driftnets the others followed suit.

5. Cost factors associated with waste disposal, or reductions in material usage force firms to modify their behavior.

Firms may also use Green Marketing in an attempt to address cost or profit related issues. Disposing of environmentally harmful by-products, such as **polychlorinated biphenyl (PCB)** contaminated oil is becoming increasingly costly and difficult. Therefore firms that can reduce harmful wastes may incur substantial cost savings. When attempting to minimize waste, firms are often forced to re-examine their production processes. In these cases they often develop more effective production processes that not only reduce waste, but reduce the need for some raw materials. This serves as a double cost savings, sine both waste and raw materials are reduced.

(Adapted from Michael Jay Polonsky: An Introduction to Green Marketing, *Electronic Green Journal,* 1(2), 1994.)

Notes

① clamshell packaging: 蛤壳式塑料包装（指用塑料做成成型的外观，产品放入成型的塑料容器内可以很好地保持其形状。但是生产塑料的主要原料及添加剂等会对臭氧层造成破坏）

② polystyrene: 聚苯乙烯，简称PS（这是一种无色透明的热塑性塑料，具有高于100摄氏度的玻璃转化温度，因此经常被用来制作各种需要承受开水的温度的一次性容器以及一次性泡沫饭盒等。聚苯乙烯制造的餐盒降解周期极长，在普通环境下可达200年左右。也就是说，在很漫长的一段岁月里，它将"我行我素"，保持自己的高分子形态不变。因此它不仅会破坏环境，而且会给人类的生存带来了较大的危害）

③ ozone depletion: 臭氧层的损耗（臭氧层被大量损耗后，吸收紫外辐射的能力大大减弱，导致到达地球表面的紫外线明显增加，给人类健康和生态环境带来多方面的危害。聚苯乙烯泡沫中的发泡剂会对臭氧层造成破坏）

④ driftnet fishing: 流网捕鱼（流网是一种很长的刺网，长达好几公里，在海里飘着，只要经过的鱼类几乎都会被伤到）

⑤ recycled photocopier paper: 可回收的复印纸

⑥ polychlorinated biphenyl (PCB): 多氯联苯（多氯联苯为联苯分子中的氢被氯取代所得的化合物。因氯取代氢的数目和位置不同而会有多种同系物和异构体。工业上用于载热体、塑料及橡胶的软化剂，油漆、油墨的添加剂以及电器中作绝缘油。PCB 物理化学性质稳定，在环境中残留期长，并可通过食物链富集，蓄积在脂肪组织中。PCB 可锈导微粒体酶，并且有抑制免疫功能、促生肿瘤及生殖毒性，被列为人类可疑致癌化合物。1968 年日本发生的米糠油中毒事件，就是由于 PCB 用作脱臭工艺的热载体而混入米糠油所引起的）

Exercises

Questions

1. Why are firms adopting the Green Marketing strategy?

2. Do you know any policy issued by the Chinese government to regulate organizations' environmental behavior?

Activity 1

Problems of Going Green

Although adopting the Green Marketing concept is a trend in the business world, some problems occur when taking the green marketing approach. Look at the following table, discuss the problems with your classmates and try to figure out solutions.

Problems	Your Solutions
1. Company A has launched a new washing machine to the market. It claims that the washing machine uses no washing powder, and can increase the cleaning capacity by 25% over ordinary machines, at the same time, it can save 50% of water and electricity. It also claims that the cleaning function is achieved by the electrolyzation of water（电解水）, a new technology. Thus this new product is sold at 1,000 RMB more than the ordinary machines. However, one day a consumer found out that the washing machine is not operating as it is claimed. Instead of putting washing powder in by consumers, the new machine uses a preinstalled surface active agent which is the raw material for producing detergent.	As a consumer, would you feel cheated? How would you solve the problem?

Problems	Your Solutions
2. The phosphate-free laundry detergent powder is more expensive than the ordinary ones in the market. Many price sensitive consumers just buy the cheaper ones.	How would you solve the problem?
3. While bringing convenience to human beings, cars also cause lots of environmental problems, such as noise, exhaust fumes, energy consumption, ozone depletion.	Can you think of some green ways to improve the cars?

 Activity 2

The Problem of Going Green is People

1. Put the right word in its right form in the right blank.

| 1. climate | 2. unsustainable | 3. current | 4. chemicals |
| 5. need | 6. energy | 7. turn off | 8. fossil fuel |

People want an easy life—they want material goods at the cheapest price, they want to use energy hungry gadgets, and they don't want to have to deal with long term consequences. All this adds up to a very _____ way of life.

"Sustainable" is a bit of a buzzword, but a sustainable way of life can be easily summarized as one in which our current needs can be met without compromising meeting the _____ of those in the future.

Our _____ way of life involves a huge expenditure of energy in order to meet our wants—and to meet this energy demand we use fossil fuels. _____ are very good at what they do—they contain high amounts of stored energy in quite a compact form. But unfortunately in burning them, we release _____ into the atmosphere which have built up to such high concentrations that they are starting to have a measurable effect on our _____.

Clearly something has to be done. We need to both find 'greener' energy sources, and reduce the amounts of _____ we use.

There are easy ways to reduce your energy consumption. _____ lights in empty rooms. Use energy efficient lightbulbs. But how many people actually follow this advice?

There are more things that can be done—insulate your attic; invest in a more efficient boiler. These things require some outlay of money, but energy saved is money gained. Again, few people will do this.

2. Put the paragraphs A, B, C, D, E and F below in the right order so that they can form a coherent article. The first paragraph is set for you.

Is Going Green the Answer?

Severe drought, global food shortages, strip-mining, the destruction of rainforests—these are a few of the issues raised by the green movement.

A: Some issues rely on science, others on ethics and morals. However, while many of the above points may be valid, will "going green" solve the world's problems?

B: It seems that everywhere you turn, the green movement asks, "Are you doing your part?"

C: The green movement asserts that the average man or women lives a life of excess: water is being used up and polluted, and fast—the global population is 6.65 billion and expected to surpass 9 billion by 2050—experts insist consumers buy organic foods so future generations will be able to continue farming—30% of wildlife species have been driven to extinction over the past 30 years.

D: Certainly, "going green" has garnered a lot of press. Virtually everywhere you turn you see "green". Major TV networks "go green" for a week, featuring shows with an environmentalist message or promoting sustainable practices. While shopping at a mall, you hear an announcement crackle over the loud speaker concerning an "eco-friendly" promotional giveaway. "Thank you for going green with us." the message ends.

E: Even though it began as a grassroots idea, going green is quickly gaining a voice. Many are looking to this movement as the way to solve man's environmental issues. But has mankind already pushed the earth past its limits—or is there still time to change if humanity comes together and acts quickly?

F: There are websites where you can take a test to see how many "earths" your lifestyle consumes. These ask about your car, job, eating habits, etc., and reveal whether you are living a sustainable lifestyle. Even if you are living under the global average, you are still reminded that we only have one earth.

Activity 3

Translation and Discussion (16)

Translate the following story and the questions into English, and then discuss the questions in English.

由于环境问题日益突出,许多企业在产品的设计、生产、包装、分销等环节开展绿色营销，并把绿色营销作为树立企业形象的一个重要手段。三个年轻人的环保意识都很强，也正在考虑如何把绿色营销的理念运用到自己的企业经营中。

问题
1. 服装的生产和销售在哪些环节涉及环保问题？
2. 请你为服装店的绿色营销设计一个宣传口号和一个以环保为主题的公关活动。

Supplementary Material

Will Green Marketing Save the Planet?

—*Anja Schaefer*

The idea of green marketing is that there is a sizeable market segment of green consumers who are willing to pay a little more for environmentally friendly products from environmentally friendly companies. Producers and retailers will react to this green demand and environmentally friendly practices will be pushed through the supply chain. Green marketing dates back several decades now, with specialist manufacturers and retailers such as **Patagonia**, **Ben and Jerry's**, **The Body Shop** and so forth, leading the way.

But there are problems with this nice idea of greening the world through marketing. And that's not even so much that companies do it in order to increase sales or profits. Of course they do. They are not charities, after all.

The biggest problem is that expecting consumer demand to drive a green revolution may not work. There is no doubt a (small) segment of dedicated green consumers who will go to significant lengths in order to inform themselves about the environmental footprint of their consumption and to reduce this as much as possible. But how many consumers will really be able to interpret carbon footprints on product information, even if **Tesco's** actually manage to calculate these with any degree of accuracy? And that is only one environmental issue to worry about. In addition there are things like packaging, organic production, sustainable resource use, and so on and so forth. It's all a bit much for the average consumer even to get interested in, never mind knowledgeable about.

And, if taken to natural conclusions, green consumption would surely require some sacrifices, i.e., no strawberries in winter, less cod and many more. Can we really expect millions of individuals to make these decisions for themselves so that the green demand then can trickle through the supply chain? More likely it would at least require some concerted action from consumers, government and industry to start tackling the problem. Market forces alone may not solve it.

About the author

Anja Schaefer is a Lecturer in Management at the Open University Business School. She's been lecturing in marketing and corporate social responsibility for eight years. Anja has published material on consumer behavior, sustainable consumption and corporate environmental management.

Notes

① Patagonia: 美国生产户外服装的公司。该公司非常注重环境保护与资源节约，总部所有的电力均来自室外大片的太阳能电池板。在全球率先为自己征收地球税，即把在全球各地的销售额的1%用于当地的地球保护。迄今PATAGONIA已捐出了4,000多万美元的"地球税"。在资源节约方面，PATAGONIA最早在美国发起资源再生的号召，把上千吨的可乐瓶回收制造新材料服装，同时提出反对使用会使土地恶化让人致癌的化肥和农药。PATAGONIA所用的棉花均是天然无害的绿色生态棉。正因PATAGONIA积极倡导环保绿色的理念，使得包括美国总统克林顿在内的政治家和演艺明星均以拥有PATAGONIA服装为荣。

② Ben and Jerry's: 美国第二大冰淇淋制造商，以倡导环保著称。

③ The Body Shop: 英国著名的健康及美容品连锁店。THE BODY SHOP自创办以来坚持五个信念：反对动物实验、支持社区公平交易、唤醒自觉意识、悍卫人权和保护地球。在此基础上为了满足各种顾客的需求开发了上千种绿色美容保养品。

④ Tesco: 英国最大的食品零售公司，目前在全球有超过2400家店，遍布英国、爱尔兰、中欧及亚洲各国。

⑤ carbon footprint: 碳排放。碳排放是关于温室气体排放的一个总称或简称。温室气体中最主要的气体是二氧化碳，因此用碳(carbon)一词作为代表。多数科学家和政府承认温室气体已经并将继续为地球和人类带来灾难，所以"控制碳排放"成为本世纪初最重要的环保话题之一。

Questions

1. Green consumption requires some sacrifice. Can you give some examples?
2. What can we do to save the Planet?